Use Both Sides of Your Brain

Other books by Tony Buzan:

Speed Memory
Speed Reading
Spore One
Advanced Learning and Reading – Manual
   (with Bernard Chibnall)
The Evolving Brain
   (with Terry Dixon)
Make the Most of Your Mind

Use Both Sides of Your Brain

REVISED AND UPDATED EDITION

TONY BUZAN

A Dutton Paperback

E. P. DUTTON, INC.   NEW YORK

Acknowledgment: the Illustration on page 12 is from "The organisation of the brain" (page 102) by Walle J. H. Nauta and Michael Feirtag, copyright © September 1979 by SCIENTIFIC AMERICAN Inc. All rights reserved.

The Illustrations on pages 12, 13 and 97–100 were drawn by Lorraine Gill.

Published in the United States by E. P. Dutton, Inc.,
2 Park Avenue, New York, N.Y. 10016

Library of Congress Catalog Card Number 82-74482

ISBN: 0-525-48011-0

10 9 8 7 6 5 4 3 2 1

First Edition

dedicated
to
YOU

and
to my beloved
Mum and Dad,
Jean and Gordon Buzan

With thanks to all those whose effort and
co-operation enabled me to write this book:

Zita Albes; Astrid Andersen; Jeannie Beattie;
Nick Beytes; Mark Brown; Joy Buttery;
my brother, Barry Buzan; Bernard Chibnall;
Steve and Fanny Colling;
Susan Crockford; Tricia Date; Charles Elton;
Lorraine Gill; Bill Harris;
Brian Helweg-Larsen;
Thomas Jarlov; Trish Lillis; Hermione Lovell;
Annette McGee; Joe McMahon;
Khalid Ranjah; Auriol Roberts;
Ian Rosenbloom;
Caitrina Ni Shuilleabhain;
Robert Millard Smith; Chris and Pat Stevens;
Jan Streit; Christopher Tatham;
Lee Taylor; Nancy Thomas; Sue Vaudin;
Jim Ward; Bill Watts; Gillian Watts.

Contents

Noting of current knowledge on the subject being studied
Planning approach to the new subject
Defining reasons for study and goals to be achieved

Introduction

This volume is written to help you do just that. By the time you have finished the book you should understand much more about how your mind works and how to use it to the best advantage, be able to read faster and more efficiently, to study more effectively, to solve problems more readily and to increase the power of your memory.

This introductory section gives general guide lines about the book's contents, and the ways in which these contents are best approached.

The chapters

Each chapter deals with a different aspect of your brain's functioning. First the book outlines the most up-to-date information about the brain and then applies this information to the way in which your vision can be best used.

Next, a chapter explains how you can improve memory both during and after learning. In addition a special system is introduced for the perfect memorisation of listed items.

The middle chapters explore the brain's internal 'maps'. This information about how you think is applied to the way in which you can use language, words and imagery for recording, organising, remembering, creative thinking and problem solving.

The last chapters deal with the new Organic Study Method which will enable you to study any subject ranging from English to Higher Mathematics.

In the centre of the book you will find mind maps which you are advised to look at before reading each chapter – they serve as a preview/review summary.

Your effort

It is essential that you practise if you wish to be able to use effectively the methods and information outlined. At various stages in the book there are exercises and suggestions for further activity.

In addition you should work out your own practice and study schedule, keeping to it as firmly as possible.

Personal notes

At the end of each chapter you will find pages for 'Personal Notes'. These are for any odd jottings you might wish to make during reading and can also be used when you discover relevant information after you have 'finished' the book.

Bibliography

On page 152 you will find a special list of books. These are not just books of academic reference, but include books which will help you develop your general knowledge as well as giving you more specialised information concerning some of the areas covered in this volume.

The Time-Life books give clear and graphic accounts of such topics as Vision and the Mind, and can be used most effectively for family reading and study.

My own book, *Speed memory,* is a combination of the special memory techniques for recalling lists, numbers, names and faces, etc. It should be used in conjunction with the information from the Memory chapter.

You and yourself

It is hoped that this volume will help you to expand as an individual, and that through an increasing awareness of yourself you will be able to develop your own ways of thinking.

Each person using information from this book starts with different levels of learning ability, and will progress at the pace best suited to him. It is important therefore to measure improvement in relation to yourself and not to others.

Although much of the information has been presented in connection with reading, formal noting and studying, the complete application is much wider. When you have finished and reviewed the book, browse through it again to see in which other areas of your life the information can be helpfully applied.

I.
Your mind is better than you think

Fig 1 **The brain**
Source: SCIENTIFIC AMERICAN (see acknowledgements for details)

Since I wrote the introductory chapter on the brain for the first edition of this volume in 1974, research in that area has been exploding with new and exciting discoveries. Rather than stating, as I did then, that 'only in the last 150 years' has the bulk of progress been made in this area, I can now state that only in the last *ten* years has the bulk of our knowledge been accumulated. This seems extraordinarily late when you consider that homosapiens appeared on earth 3,500,000 years ago. Bear in mind, however, that mankind has only known the *location* of its brain for the last 500 years. In some ways this is not surprising. Consider for a moment that you have no idea where your brain is to be found, and a friend asks: 'Where is the centre of your feelings, emotions, thoughts, memories, drives and desires located?'. You, like most others (including Aristotle!) might quite rationally decide that your brain was located in the heart and stomach area, because that is where you experience the direct physical manifestation of mental activity most regularly and dramatically.

If, even now, as we pursue with computers and electron microscopes what must be the most elusive quarry man has ever chased, we must still admit that the sum total of the knowledge we have acquired today is probably less than 1% of what there is to know. Just when tests seem to prove that the mind works in a given way, along comes another test which proves that it doesn't work that way at all, or along comes another human being with a brain which manages to make the test meaningless.

What we *are* gathering from our efforts at the moment is a knowledge that the mind is infinitely more subtle than we previously thought, and that everyone who has what is ironically called a 'normal' mind has a much larger ability and potential than was previously thought.

A few examples will help to make this clear.

Most of the more scientific disciplines, despite their apparent differences of direction, are all being drawn into a whirlpool, the centre of which is the mind. Chemists are now involved with the intricate chemical structures that exist and interact inside our heads; biologists are struggling with the brain's biological functions; physicists are finding parallels with their investigations into the farthest reaches of space; psychologists are trying to pin the mind down and are finding the experience frustratingly like trying to place a finger on a little globule of mercury; and mathematicians who have constructed models for complex computers and even for the Universe itself, still can't come up with a formula for the operations that go on regularly inside each of our heads every day of our lives.

What we *have* discovered during the last decade is that you have two upper brains rather than one, and that they operate in very different mental areas; that the potential patterns your brain can make is even greater than was thought at the end of the 1960's, and that your brain requires very different kinds of food if it is to survive, *see fig. 2.*

In Californian laboratories in the late 1960's and early 1970's, research was begun which was to change the history of our

R   L

rhythm   language

music   logic

images   number

imagination   sequence

daydreaming   linearity

colour   analysis

dimension

Fig 2 **Front view of the two sides of your brain and their functions.**

appreciation of the human brain, and which was to eventually win Roger Sperry of the California Institute of Technology a Nobel Prize and Robert Ornstein worldwide fame for his work on brain waves and specialisation of function.

In summary, what Sperry and Ornstein discovered was that the two sides of your brain, or your two brains, which are linked by a fantastically complex network of nerve fibres called the Corpus Collosum, deal with different types of mental activity.

In most people the left side of the brain deals with logic, language, reasoning, number, linearity, and analysis etc, the so-called 'academic' activities. While the left side of the brain is engaged in these activities, the right side is in the 'alpha wave' or resting state. The right side of the brain deals with rhythm, music, images and imagination, colour, parallel processing, daydreaming, face recognition, and pattern or map recognition.

Subsequent researches showed that when people were encouraged to develop a mental area they had previously considered weak, this development, rather than detracting from other areas, seemed to produce a synergetic effect in which *all* areas of mental performance improved.

At first glance history seemed to deny this finding however, for most of the 'great brains' appeared very lopsided in mental terms: Einstein and other scientists seemed to be predominantly 'left-brain' dominant, while Picasso, Cezanne and other artists and musicians appeared to be 'right-brain' dominant.

A more thorough investigation unearthed some fascinating truths: Einstein failed mathematics at school, numbered among his other activities violin playing, art, sailing, and imagination games!

To his imagination games Einstein gave credit for many of his more significant scientific insights. While daydreaming on a hill on a summer day, he imagined riding sunbeams to the far extremities of the universe, and upon finding himself returned, 'illogically', to the surface of the sun, he realised that the universe must indeed be curved, and that his previous 'logical' training was incomplete. The numbers, formulas, equations and words he wrapped around this new image gave us the theory of relativity – a left *and* right brain synthesis.

Similarly the great artists turned out to be 'both-brained'. Rather than note books filled with stories of drunken parties, and paint slapped haphazardly to produce masterpieces, entries similar to the following were found:

'Up at 6 am. Spent seventeenth day on painting six of the latest series. Mixed four parts orange with two parts yellow to produce colour combination which I placed in upper left-hand corner of canvas, to act in visual opposition to spiral structures in lower right-hand corner, producing desired balance in eye of perceiver.' – Telling examples of just how much left-brain activity goes into what we normally consider right-brain pursuits.

In addition to the researches of Sperry and Ornstein, the experimental evidence of increased overall performance, and the confirming historical fact that many of the 'great brains' were indeed using both ranges of their capacity, one man in the last thousand years stands out as a supreme example of what a single human being can do if both sides of the brain are developed simultaneously: Leonardo da Vinci. In his time he was arguably the most accomplished man in *each* of the following disciplines: art, sculpture, physiology, general science, architecture, mechanics, anatomy, physics, and invention. Rather than separating these different areas of his latent ability, he *combined* them. Leonardo's scientific note books are filled with 3-dimensional drawings and images; but perhaps more interestingly, the final plans for his great painting masterpieces often look like architectural plans: straight lines, angles, curves and numbers.

It seems, then, that when we describe ourselves as talented in certain areas and not talented in others, what we are *really* describing is those areas of our potential that we have successfully developed, and those areas of our potential that still lie dormant, which in reality could, with the right nurturing, flourish.

The right and left brain findings give added support to the work you will be doing on memory systems, on note taking and communication, and on advanced mind mapping techniques, for in each of these areas it is essential to use *both* sides of your brain.

As an addendum, it is interesting to note that Dr David Samuels of the Weizmann Institute estimated that underlying the brain's basic range of activities, there are between 100,000 and 1,000,000 different chemical reactions taking place every minute!

We also know that in an average brain there are 10,000,000,000 individual neurons or nerve cells. This figure became even more astounding when it was realised that each neuron can interact with other neurons in not just one, but many ways – At the time I was writing the first edition of this volume in 1974, it had been recently estimated that the number of interconnections might be as many as 10 with eight hundred noughts following it. To realise just how enormous this number is, compare it with a mathematical fact about the Universe: one of the smallest items in the Universe is the atom. The biggest thing we know is the Universe itself. The number of atoms in the Universe is predictably enormous: 10 with one hundred noughts after it. The number of interconnections in *one* brain makes even this number seem tiny. *See figs 3 and 4.*

Shortly after the first edition of this volume was published, Dr Pyotra Anokin of Moscow University, who had spent the last few years of his life studying the information processing capabilities of the brain, stated that the number one followed by 800 noughts was a gross under-estimation, that the new number he had calculated was conservative due to the relative clumsiness of our current measuring instruments in comparison to the incredible delicacy of the brain, and that the number was

10,000,000,000,000,000,000,000,000,000,000,000,000,000,000,000,000,000,000,000,000,000,000,000,000,000,000,000,000,000,000,000,000,000,000

Fig 3 The number of atoms (one of the smallest particles we know of) in the known universe (the largest thing we know of). *See text on facing page.*

10,000,000,000,000,000,000,000,000,000,000,000,000,000,
000,000,000,000,000,000,000,000,000,000,000,000,000,000,
000,000,000,000,000,000,000,000,000,000,000,000,000,000,
000,000,000,000,000,000,000,000,000,000,000,000,000,000,
000,000,000,000,000,000,000,000,000,000,000,000,000,000,
000,000,000,000,000,000,000,000,000,000,000,000,000,000,
000,000,000,000,000,000,000,000,000,000,000,000,000,000,
000,000,000,000,000,000,000,000,000,000,000,000,000,000,
000,000,000,000,000,000,000,000,000,000,000,000,000,000,
000,000,000,000,000,000,000,000,000,000,000,000,000,000,
000,000,000,000,000,000,000,000,000,000,000,000,000,000,
000,000,000,000,000,000,000,000,000,000,000,000,000,000,
000,000,000,000,000,000,000,000,000,000,000,000,000,000,
000,000,000,000,000,000,000,000,000,000,000,000,000,000,
000,000,000,000,000,000,000,000,000,000,000,000,000,000,
000,000,000,000,000,000,000,000,000,000,000,000,000,000,
000,000,000,000,000,000,000,000,000,000,000,000,000,000,
000,000,000,000,000,000,000,000,000,000,000,000,000,000,
000,000,000,000,000,000,000,000,000,000,000,000,000,000,
000,000,000,000,000,000,000,000,000,000,000,000,000,000,
000,000

Fig 4 In the late 1960's it was calculated that the number of different patterns that the 10,000,000,000 individual nerve cells of the brain could make was this number followed by 800 noughts. Recent estimates have shown that even this number is too small! *See text on facing page.*

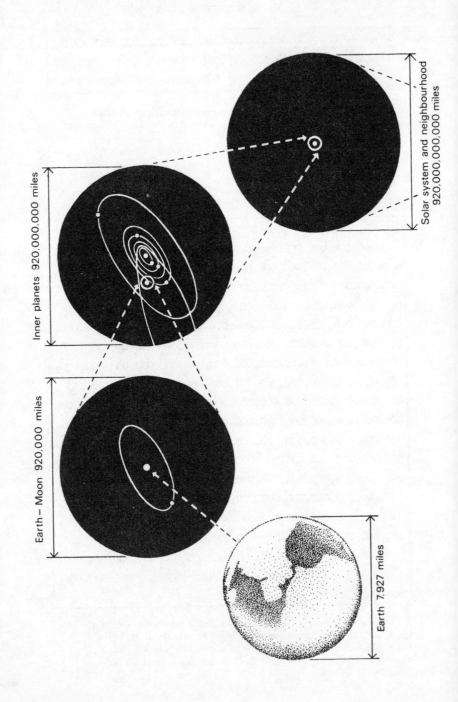

Inner planets 920,000,000 miles

Solar system and neighbourhood 920,000,000,000 miles

Earth – Moon 920,000 miles

Earth 7,927 miles

Nearest stars
920,000,000,000,000 miles

Our galaxy (the Milky Way)
920,000,000,000,000,000,000,000 miles

Nearby galaxies
920,000,000,000,000,000,000,000,000,000,000 miles

14

Fig 5 The enormous size of the known universe. Each successive black sphere is a thousand million times (1,000,000,000) as big as the one before it. *See text pages 16 and 20*

Fig 6 **The atom – one of the tiniest entities known. In the tip of a person's finger there are many billions of atoms, and in the entire universe a number equal to 10 with 100 noughts after it.**
For the relationship between these facts and the brain's interconnecting networks, see Figs 3 and 4 and text pages 16 and 20.

not one, followed by 800 noughts, but that the pattern-making capability of the brain, or 'degrees of freedom' throughout the brain is 'so great that writing it would take a line of figures, in normal manuscript characters, more than 10.5 million kilometres in length! With such a number of possibilities, the brain is a keyboard on which hundreds of millions of different melodies – acts of behaviour or intelligence – can be played.'

Other examples of the mind's abilities abound – examples of extraordinary memory feats, feats of super-strength, and unusual control of body functions defying the 'laws of science', are becoming more widespread. They are now fortunately more documented, generally recognised and usefully applied.

Even with the mounting evidence a number of people still remain sceptical, pointing to the performance of most of us as a contradiction of that evidence. In response to this objection a questionnaire was given to people from all areas of life to determine why this amazing organ is so under-used. The questions are noted below, and underneath each question is noted the reply given by at least 95 per cent. As you read ask yourself the questions.

- **In school were you taught anything about your brain and how understanding its functions could help you learn, memorise, think, etc?**
  No
- **Were you taught anything about how your memory functions?**
  No.

- Were you taught anything about special and advanced memory techniques?
  No.
- Anything about how your eye functions when you are learning, and about how you can use this knowledge to your advantage?
  No.
- Anything about the ranges of study techniques and how they can be applied to different disciplines?
  No.
- Anything about the nature of concentration and how to maintain it when necessary?
  No.
- Anything about motivation, how it effects your abilities, and how you can use it to your advantage?
  No.
- Anything about the nature of key words and key concepts and how they relate to note taking and imagination etc?
  No.
- Anything about thinking?
  No.
- Anything about creativity?
  No.

By now the answer to the original objection should be clear: the reasons why our performances do not match even our minimum potentials is that we are given no information about what we are, or about how we can best utilise our inherent capacities.

A similar reply can be given to those who say that IQ tests measure our 'absolute intelligence' so therefore *they* must be right.

Apart from the fact that an IQ score can be significantly changed by even a small amount of well-directed practice, there are other arguments against these tests:

First the Berkeley Study on Creativity showed that a person whose IQ assessment was high was not necessarily independent in thought; independent in action; either possessed of or able to value a good sense of humour; appreciative of beauty; reasonable; relativistic; able to enjoy complexity and novelty; original; comprehensively knowledgeable; fluent; flexible; or astute.

Secondly, those who argue that IQ does measure a wide and absolute range of human abilities have failed to consider that the test should be concerned with three major areas: 1: the brain being tested; 2: the test itself; 3: the results. Unfortunately the IQ protagonists have become too obsessed with the test and the results and have neglected the real nature of the brain being tested.

They have failed to realise that their tests do not test basic human ability, but measure untrained and undeveloped human performance. Their claims are much like those of an imaginary surveyor of women's feet sizes in the Orient at the time when their feet were restricted to make them small. From the crib the foot was placed in bandages until the woman was nearly full grown. This was done to stunt the growth and to produce 'dainty' feet.

To assume, however, as the surveyor might have done, that these measurements represent natural and fully developed bodily dimensions is as absurd as it is to assume that intelligence tests measure the natural dimensions of our minds. Our minds, like the women's feet, have been 'bound' by the way we have misjudged and mistrained them, and are therefore not naturally developed.

Another most convincing case for the excellence of the human brain, is the functioning and development of the human baby. Far from being the 'helpless and incapable little thing' that many people assume it to be, it is the most extraordinary learning, remembering and intellectually advanced being – even in its most early stages it surpasses the performance of the most sophisticated computers.

With very few exceptions, all babies learn to speak by the time they are two, and many even earlier. Because this is so universal it is taken for granted, but if the process is examined more closely it is seen to be extremely complex.

Try listening to someone speaking while pretending that you have no knowledge of language and very little knowledge of the objects and ideas the language discusses. Not only will this task be difficult, but because of the way sounds run into each other the distinction between different words will often be totally unclear. Every baby who has learned to talk has overcome not only these difficulties but also the difficulties of sorting out what makes sense and what doesn't. When he is confronted with sounds like 'koooochiekooochiekoooooooooaahhhhisn'tealovelelyli'ldarling!' one wonders how he ever manages to make sense of us at all!

The young child's ability to learn language involves him in processes which include a subtle control of, and an inherent understanding of, rhythm, mathematics, music, physics, linguistics, spatial relations, memory, integration, creativity, logical reasoning and thinking – left and right brains working from the word go.

The reader who still doubts his own abilities has himself learned to talk and to read. He should therefore find it difficult to attack a position of which he himself is evidence for the defence.

There really is no doubt that the brain is capable of infinitely more complex tasks than has been thought. The remainder of this book will attempt to shed light on a number of the areas in which performance and self-realisation can be achieved.

Personal Notes

2.
Reading more efficiently and faster

Overview

- Reading and learning problems
- Reading and learning –
  definition – the process
- Misconceptions about reading and
  speed reading; why they arose
- The eye
- Perception during reading and learning
- Exercises for improving comprehension
  and speed

Reading and learning problems

In the space below note *all* the problems you have with reading and learning. Be strict with yourself. The more you are able to define, the more completely you will be able to improve.

Note your own definition of the word *Reading*.

Teachers of reading and learning have noted over the past five years that in each of their classes, the same general problems arise. Below is the list of those most commonly experienced. The reader is advised to check his own against these, adding to his own list any others that apply – there will probably be quite a few.

vision	fatigue	recall
speed	laziness	impatience
comprehension	boredom	vocabulary
time	interest	subvocalisation
amount	analysis	typography
surroundings	criticism	literary style
noting	motivation	selection
retention	appreciation	rejection
age	organisation	concentration
fear	regression	back-skipping

Each of the problems in the table above is serious, and can by itself disrupt reading and learning. This book is devoted to solving these problems, the current chapter being concerned primarily with vision, speed, comprehension, time and amount, and the learning environment.

Before getting down to the more physical aspects of reading I shall first define the term properly, and in the light of this definition shall explain why the wide range of problems that exist is so universally experienced.

Reading defined

Reading, which is often defined as 'getting from the book what the author intended' or 'assimilating the written word' deserves a far more complete definition. It can be defined as follows: Reading is the individual's total interrelationship with symbolic information. It is usually the visual aspect of learning, and contains the following seven steps:

recognition

The reader's knowledge of the alphabetic symbols.
This step takes place almost before the physical aspect
of reading begins.

assimilation

The physical process by which light is reflected from
the word and is received by the eye, then transmitted
via the optic nerve to the brain. *See fig 39.*

intra-integration

The equivalent to basic understanding, and refers to
the linking of all parts of the information being read
with all other appropriate parts.

extra-integration

This includes analysis, criticism, appreciation,
selection and rejection. The process in which the
reader brings the whole body of his previous
knowledge to the new knowledge he is reading, making
the appropriate connections.

retention

The basic storage of information. Storage can itself
become a problem. Most readers will have experienced
entering an examination room and storing most of their
information during the two hour exam period! Storage,
then, is not enough in itself, and must be accompanied
by recall.

recall

The ability to get back out of storage that which is
needed, preferably *when* it is needed.

communication

The use to which the information is immediately or
eventually put; includes the very important subdivision:
thinking.

The definition includes consideration of most of the problems
listed on page 27. The only problems not included are those
which are, in a sense, 'outside' the reading process, 'surroundings', 'age', etc.

Why the problems exist

The reader may justifiably ask at this point w.
experience the problems noted.

The answer, in addition to our previous lack o.
about the brain, lies in our approach to the initial teaching
ing. Most of you reading this book who are over twenty-fiv
probably have been taught by the Phonic or Alphabet Meth
Others will probably have been taught by either this or by the
Look and Say Method.

The most simplified Phonic Method teaches the child first
the alphabet, then the different sounds for each of the letters in
the alphabet, then the blending of sounds in syllables, and finally
the blending of sounds forming words. From this point on he is
given progressively more difficult books, usually in the form of
series graded 1 to 10, through which he progresses at his own
speed. He becomes a 'silent' reader during the process.

The Look and Say Methods teach the child by presenting him
with cards on which there are pictures. The names of the objects
shown are clearly printed underneath them. Once a child has become familiar with the pictures and the names associated with
them, the pictures are removed leaving only the words. When the
child has built up enough basic vocabulary he progresses
through a series of graded books similar to those for the child
taught by the Phonic Method, and also becomes a 'silent' reader.

The outlines given of the two methods are necessarily brief,
and there are at least fifty other methods similar to these pre-
sently being taught in England and in other English-speaking
countries. Similar problems exist all over the world.

The point about these methods, however, is not that they are
inadequate for achieving their aim, but that they are inadequate
for teaching any child to read in the complete sense of the word.

Referring to the definition of Reading, it can be seen that
these methods are designed to cover only the stage of recognition
in the process, with some attempt at assimilation and intra-
integration. The methods do not touch on the problems of
speed, time, amount, retention, recall, selection, rejection, note-
taking, concentration, appreciation, criticism, analyses, organisation, motivation, interest, boredom, surroundings, fatigue or
typographic style, etc.

can thus be seen that there is justification for the problems so widely experienced.

Recognition, it is important to note, is hardly ever mentioned as a problem, because it has been taught adequately in the early years of school. All the other problems are mentioned because they have *not* been dealt with during the educational process.

Later chapters deal with the majority of these problems. The remainder of this chapter is devoted to eye movement, comprehension and the speed of reading.

optic nerve

sclera

choroid

retina

conjunctiva

iris

lens

ciliary muscle

Fig 7 **Your eye.**

Reading eye movements

When asked to show with their forefinger the movement and speed of their eyes as they read most people move their fingers along in smooth lines from left to right, with a quick jump from the end of one line back to the beginning of the next. They normally take between a quarter to one second for each line.

Fig 8 **Assumed reading eye movement as shown by people with no knowledge of eye movements. Each line is thought to be covered in less than one second.** *See text this page.*

Two major errors are being made: the movement and the speed.

Even if the eye moved as slowly as one line per second, words would be covered at the rate of 600–700 words per minute (wpm). As the average reading speed on even light material is 250 wpm, it can be seen that even those estimating slower speeds assume that they cover words much more rapidly than they really do.

If eyes moved over print in the smooth manner shown above they would be able to take in nothing, because the eye can see things clearly only when it can 'hold them still'. If an object is still, the eye must be still in order to see it, and if an object is moving, the eye must move with the object in order to see it. A simple experiment either by yourself or with a friend will confirm this. Hold a forefinger motionless in front of the eyes and either feel your own eyes or watch your friend's eyes as they look at the object. They will remain still. Next move the finger up, down, sideways and around, following it with the eyes. And finally move the finger up, down and around, holding the eyes still, or cross both hands in front of your face, at the same time looking at them both simultaneously. (If you can accomplish this last feat write to me immediately!) When objects move, eyes move with them if they are to be seen clearly.

Relating all this to reading, it is obvious that if the eyes are going to take in words, and if the words are still, the eyes will have to pause on each word before moving on. Rather than moving in smooth lines as shown in fig 8, the eyes in fact move in a series of stops and quick jumps.

Fig 9 **Diagram representing the stop-and-start movement of the eyes during the reading process.** *See text this page.*

The jumps themselves are so quick as to take almost no time, but the fixations can take anywhere from ¼ to 1½ seconds. A person who normally reads one word at a time – and who skips back over words and letters is forced, by the simple mathematics of his eye movements, into reading speeds which are often well below 100 wpm, and which mean that he will not be able to understand much of what he reads, nor be able to read much.

Fig 10 **Diagram showing poor reading habits of slow reader: one word read at a time, with unconscious back-skipping, visual wandering, and conscious regressions.** *See text this page.*

It might seem at first glance that the slow reader is doomed, but the problem can be solved, and in more than one way:

1 Skipping back over words can be eliminated, as 90 per cent of back-skipping and regression is based on apprehension and is unnecessary for understanding. The 10 per cent of words that

do need to be reconsidered can be noted as explained in the chapter on Organic Study, page 117.

2 The time for each fixation can be reduced to approach the ¼ second minimum – the reader need not fear that this is too short a time, for his eye is able to register as many as five words in one one-hundredth of a second.

3 The size of the fixation can be expanded to take in as many as three to five words at a time.

Fig 11 Diagram showing eye movements of a better and more efficient reader. More words are taken in at each fixation, and back-skipping, regression and visual wandering are reduced.

This solution might at first seem impossible if it is true that the mind deals with one word at a time. In fact it can equally well fixate on *groups* of words, which is better in nearly all ways: When we read a sentence we do not read it for the individual meaning of each word, but for the meaning of the phrases in which the words are contained.

Reading for example, the   cat
                sat   on   the
road is more difficult than reading the cat sat   on the road.

The slower reader has to do more mental work than the faster more smooth reader because he has to add the meaning of each word to the meaning of each following word. In the above example this amounts to five or six additions. The more efficient reader, absorbing in meaningful units, has only one simple addition.

Another advantage for the faster reader is that his eyes will be doing less physical work on each page. Rather than having as many as 500 fixations tightly focused per page as does the slow reader, he will have as few as 100 fixations per page, each one of which is less muscularly fatiguing.

Yet another advantage is that the rhythm and flow of the faster reader will carry him comfortably through the meaning, whereas the slow reader, because of his stopping and starting, jerky approach, will be far more likely to become bored, to lose concentration, to mentally drift away and to lose the meaning of what he his reading.

It can be seen from this that a number of the commonly held beliefs about faster readers are false:

1 **Words must be read one at a time:** *Wrong.* Because of our ability to fixate and because we read for meaning rather than for single words.

2 **Reading faster than 500 wpm is impossible:** *Wrong.* Because the fact that we can take in as many as six words per fixation and the fact that we can make four fixations a second means that speeds of 1,000 wpm are perfectly feasible.

3 **The faster reader is not able to appreciate:** *Wrong.* Because the faster reader will be understanding more of the meaning of what he reads, will be concentrating on the material more, and will have considerably more time to go back over areas of special interest and importance to him.

4 **Higher speeds give lower concentration:** *Wrong.* Because the faster we go the more impetus we gather and the more we concentrate.

5 **Average reading speeds are natural and therefore the best:** *Wrong.* Because average reading speeds are not natural. They are speeds produced by an incomplete initial training in reading, combined with an inadequate knowledge of how the eye and brain work at the various speeds possible.

Advanced reading techniques

Apart from the general advice given above, some readers may be able to benefit from the following information which is usually practised in conjunction with a qualified instructor:

1 **Visual aid techniques:** When children learn how to read they often point with their finger to the words they are reading. We have traditionally regarded this as a fault and have told them to

take their fingers off the page. It is now realised that it is we and not the children who are at fault. Instead of insisting that they remove their fingers we should ask them to move their fingers faster. It is obvious that the hand does not slow down the eye, and the added values that the aid gives in establishing a smooth rhythmical habit are immeasurable.

To observe the difference between unaided and aided eye movement, ask a friend to imagine a large circle about one foot in front of him, and then ask him to look slowly and carefully around the circumference. Rather than moving in a perfect circle, his eyes will follow a pattern more resembling an arthritic rectangle.

Fig. 12 **Pattern showing unaided eye movement attempting to move around the circumference of a circle.** *See text this page.*

Next trace a circle in the air with your finger asking your friend to follow the tip of your finger as you move smoothly around the circumference. You will observe that the eyes will follow almost perfectly and will trace a circle similar to that shown below.

Fig 13 **Pattern showing aided eye movement around the circumference of a circle.** *See text this page.*

This simple experiment also indicates what an enormous improvement in performance there can be if a person is given the basic information about the physical function of the eye and brain. In many instances no long training or arduous practising is necessary. The results, as in this case, are immediate.

The reader is not restricted to the use of his forefinger as a visual aid, and can use to advantage a pen or a pencil, as many naturally efficient readers do. At first the visual aid will make the reading speed look slow. This is because, as mentioned earlier, we all imagine that we read a lot faster than we actually do. But the aided reading speed will actually be faster.

2 **Expanded focus.** In conjunction with visual aid techniques, the reader can practise taking in more than one line at a time. This is certainly not physically impossible and is especially useful on light material or for overviewing and previewing. It will also improve normal reading speeds. It is very important always to use a visual guide during this kind of reading, as without it the eye will tend to wander with comparatively little direction over the page. Various patterns of visual aiding should be experimented with, including diagonal, curving, and straight-down-the-page movements.

3 **High speed perception.** This exercise involves turning pages as fast as possible attempting to see as many words per page as possible. This form of training will increase the ability to take in large groups of words per fixation, will be applicable to overviewing and previewing techniques, and will condition the mind to much more rapid and efficient general reading practices. This high speed conditioning can be compared to driving along a motorway at 90 miles an hour for one hour. Imagine you had been driving at this speed, and you suddenly came to a road sign saying 'slow to 30'. To what speed would you slow down if somebody covered your speedometer and said 'go on, tell me when you reach 30'. The answer of course would be 50 or 60 mph.

The reason for this is that the mind has become conditioned to a much higher speed, which becomes 'normal'. Previous 'normals' are more or less forgotten in the presence of the new ones.

Fig 14 **Illustration showing how the mind 'gets used to' speed and motion. The same kind of relativistic 'misjudgements' can be used to advantage to help us learn to learn more adequately.** *See text pages 36 and 37.*

The same applies to reading, and after a high speed practice you will often find yourself reading at twice the speed without even feeling the difference. *See fig 14.*

Motivational practice

Most reading is done at a relaxed and almost lackadaisical pace, a fact of which many speed reading courses have taken advantage. Students are given various exercises and tasks, and it is suggested to them that after each exercise their speed will increase by 10–20 wpm. And so it does, often by as much as 100 per cent over the duration of the lessons. The increase, however, is often due not to the exercises, but to the fact that the student's motivation has been eked out bit by bit during the course.

The same significant increases could be produced by guaranteeing each student, at the beginning of the course, the fulfilment of any wish he desired. Performance would immediately equal those normally achieved at the end of such courses – similar to the unathletic fellow who runs a hundred metres in 10 seconds flat and jumps a six-foot fence when being chased by a bull. In these cases motivation is the major factor, and the reader will benefit enormously by consciously applying it to each learning experience. If a deep-rooted decision is made to do better, then poor performance will automatically improve.

Metronome training

A metronome, which is usually used for keeping musical rhythm, can be most useful for both reading and high speed reading practices. If you set it at a reasonable pace, each beat can indicate a single sweep for your visual aid. In this way a steady and smooth rhythm can be maintained and the usual slowdown that occurs after a little while can be avoided. Once the most comfortable rhythm has been found, your reading speed can be improved by occasionally adding an extra beat per minute.

The metronome can also be used to pace the high speed perception exercises, starting at slower rates and accelerating to exceptionally fast rates, 'looking' at one page per beat.

The information on eye movements, visual aids and advanced reading techniques should be applied by the reader to each of his reading situations. It will be found that these techniques and items of advice will become more useful when applied together with information and techniques from other chapters, especially the last three dealing with the Organic Study Method.

At the end of this chapter are a series of exercises which give practice in all areas. These exercises should be done in 5 to 20-minute sessions per day, preferably before any normal reading or studying. During the first few weeks as much as half-an-hour per day can be spent profitably. As you become more practised in the exercises they need be done only when revision is felt necessary.

NB The formula for working out speed in wpm is:

wpm (speed) =

$$\frac{\text{number of pages read} \times \text{number of words per average page}}{\text{number of minutes spent reading}}$$

Exercises

NB After any wpm calculation enter the number on the graph on page 40.

1 Exercise eye movements over page, moving eyes on horizontal and vertical planes diagonally upper left to lower right, and then upper right to lower left. Speed up gradually day by day. Purpose – to train eyes to function more accurately and independently.

2 Read normally for 5 minutes from a book which you will be able to continue using. Record wpm on continuing graph page 40.

3 Practise turning 100 pages at approximately 2 seconds per page, moving eyes very rapidly down the page. (2×2 min. sessions).

4 a Practise as fast as you can for 1 minute, not worrying about comprehension.
   b Read with motivated comprehension – 1 minute.
   c Calculate and record wpm on graph.
Repeat as time allows.

5 Use any book (light material) of your choice, preferably one in which you are interested.
   Try for as much comprehension as possible, but realise that exercise is concerned primarily with speed. In this exercise reading should continue from last point reached.

   a Practise-read for 1 minute at 100 wpm faster than your highest normal speed.
   b Practise-read 100 wpm faster than (a).
   c Practise-read 100 wpm faster than (b).
   d Practise-read 100 wpm faster than (c).
   e Practise-read 100 wpm faster than (d).
   f Practise-read with comprehension for 1 minute from point reached at end of (e). Calculate and record wpm on graph

See exercises pages 39 and 41

This graph should soon be complete. When it is full make another similar one and keep it in your book.

6 High Speed Practice 1

   a Use any easy book. Start from the beginning of a chapter.

   b Practise-read with visual aid, three lines at a time at a *minimum* of 2,000 wpm for 5 minutes.

   c Re-read to mark in 4 minutes.

   d Re-read to mark in 3 minutes.

   e Re-read to mark in 2 minutes.

   f Read on from mark, for same comprehension as at (b) for 5 minutes.

   g Read for normal comprehension for 1 minute. Record wpm on graph.

7 High Speed Practice 2

   a Use any easy book, start at the beginning of a chapter.

   b Scan for one minute, using visual aid, 4 seconds per page.

   c Practise-read from the beginning at minimum of 2,000 wpm for 5 minutes.

   d Repeat this exercise when possible.

   e As 6g.

Personal Notes

3.
Memory

Overview

- Questions on memory
- Recall during a learning period
- Recall after a learning period
- Review techniques and theory
- The brain and ageing
- Memory systems – those used by the Greeks and still used by stage performers to astound audiences

Test 1

Below these instructions is a list of words. Read each word on this list once, quickly, in order, and then turn to page 50 and fill in as many of the words as you can. You will not be able to remember all of them, so simply try for as many as you can. Read the complete list, one after the other. To ensure you do this properly use a small card, covering each word as you read it.

start now

went

the

book

work

and

good

and

start

of

the

late

white

and

paper

Mohammed Ali

light

of

skill

the

own

stair

note

and

rode

will

time

home

Next turn to page 50 fill in as many of these items as you can, and answer the questions which immediately follow on page 50.

Test 2

On page 51 you will find a blank graph. Fill it in with a line which represents the amount you think your memory recalls during a learning period. The vertical left-hand line marks the starting point for the learning; the vertical right-hand line marks the point when learning stops; the bottom line represents no recall at all (complete forgetting); and the top line represents perfect recall.

Below are examples of graphs filled in by three people.

These graphs start at 75% because it is assumed that most standard learning does not produce 100% understanding or recall.

There are of course many other alternatives so now turn to page 51 and complete the graph for the way in which you think your recall works.

Fig 15 **Three examples of graphs filled in to indicate recall during a learning period.**

A who thought his recall of the new information he was understanding stayed constant during his learning.

B who thought he remembered more from the beginning of a learning period and less from the end.

C who thought he remembered less from the beginning and more from the end.

Test 3

On page 52 is a blank graph to show the way your memory behaves *after* a learning period has been completed. The vertical left-hand line marks the end point of your learning; there is no right-hand vertical line because it is assumed that the 'afterwards' would be for a few years!; the bottom line represents no recall at all; and the top line represents perfect recall.

The graphs below show three people's assessment of their recall after learning.

Fig 16 Three examples of graphs filled in to show recall after a learning period has been completed.

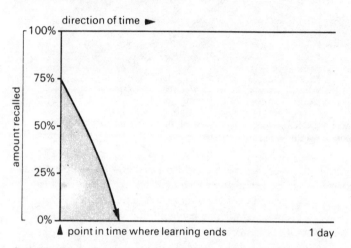

A who thought he forgot nearly everything in a very short period of time.

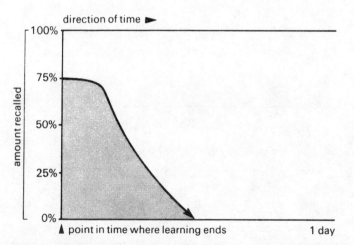

B who thought his recall was constant for a little while and then dropped off fairly steeply.

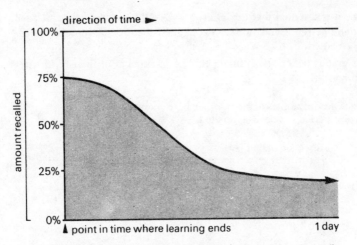

C who thought his memory stayed constant for a while and then dropped off more slowly, levelling out at a certain point.

As with Test 2 there are many alternatives, so now turn to page 52 and complete the graph in the way which most closely represents what you feel to be your normal pattern of forgetting. For the purpose of the exercise you can assume that nothing happens after your learning period to remind you of the information you learned.

Test 4

Here is a list of words next to numbers. As with Test 1 read each item once, covering the ones read with a card as you progress down the list. The purpose of this is to remember which word went with which number:

4 glass

9 mash

1 watch

6 chair

10 carpet

5 paper

8 stone

3 orange

7 banana

2 sky

Now turn to page 52 and fill in the answers in the order requested.

Test responses and further questions

Test 1: responses

When answering the questions, do not refer to the original list

1   Fill in as many of the words, in order, as you can.

word, the, and, book, work the

2   How many of the words from the beginning of the list did you remember before making the first error?

five

3   Can you recall any words which appeared more than once in the list?

if so note them

and, the

4   How many of the words within the last five did you remember?

none

5 Do you remember any item from the list which was outstandingly different from the rest?

Muhamed Ali

6 How many words from the middle of the list can you remember which you have not already noted in answers to previous questions?

looks of

Test 2: responses

Fill in, as demonstrated in the examples of *fig 15 pages 45 and 46*, the line which represents the way your memory recalls *during* a learning period.

Test 3: responses

Fill in the graph below in the way you think your recall behaves after a learning period has been completed. *See examples fig 16 pages 47 and 48.*

Test 4: responses

Here are the numbers 1 to 10. Fill in next to each number the word which originally appeared next to it. The numbers are not listed in the same order as before. Do not refer back until you have filled in as many as you can.

1	7
5	4
3	6
8	10
9	2

Score _____

Recall during learning – discussion of Tests 1 and 2

Test 1 showed how recall functions during a period of learning, as long as understanding remains fairly constant (the words in the list were not 'difficult').

In this test virtually everyone has the following results: anywhere between 2 and 8 of the words at the beginning of the list are recalled; most of the words which appear more than once are recalled (in this case 'the', 'and', 'of'); one or two of the last five words are recalled; and the outstanding word or phrase is recalled (in this case Mohammed Ali); very few of the words from the middle are recalled.

This is a pattern of test scores which shows very dramatically that memory and understanding do not work in exactly the same way as time progresses – all the words were understood, but only some were recalled. The differences between the way in which memory and understanding function help explain why so many people find they don't recall very much after hours of learning and understanding. The reason is that recall tends to get progressively worse as time goes on unless the mind is given brief rests.

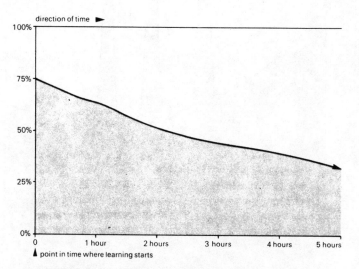

Fig 17 **As time goes on, recall of material being learned tends to get progressively worse unless the mind is given proper rests.** *See text this page.*

Thus the graph requested in Test 2 will be more complex than the simple examples given. It will probably also be more complex than the graph you have traced for your own recall behaviour during learning. Average scores from Test 1 produce a graph similar to fig 18.

From the graph it is clear that under normal circumstances and with understanding fairly constant, we tend to recall: more at the beginning and ends of learning periods; more of items which are associated by repetition, sense, rhyming etc.; more of things which are outstanding or unique; and considerably *less* of things from the middle of learning periods.

If recall is going to be kept at a reasonable level, it is necessary to find the point at which recall and understanding work in

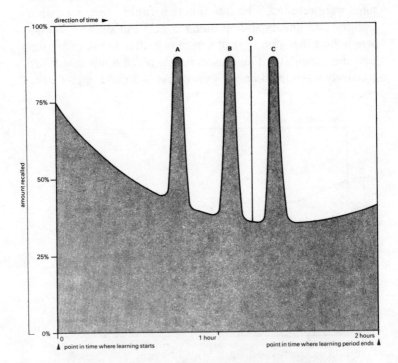

Fig 18 **Recall during learning. Graph indicating that we recall more from the beginning and ends of a learning period. We also recall more when things are associated or linked (A, B and C) and more when things are outstanding or unique (O).** *See text pages 53 and 54.*

greatest harmony. For normal purposes this point occurs in a time period of between 20 to 40 minutes. A shorter period does not give the mind enough time to appreciate the rhythm and organisation of the material, and a longer period results in the continuing decline of the amount recalled. *As graphed in fig 19.*

If a period of learning from a lecture, a book or the mass media is to take two hours, it is far better to arrange for brief breaks during these two hours. In this way the recall curve can be kept high, and can be prevented from dropping during the later stages of learning. The small breaks will guarantee eight relatively high points of recall, with four small drops in the middle. Each of the drops will be less than the main drop would have been were there no breaks. *See fig 19.*

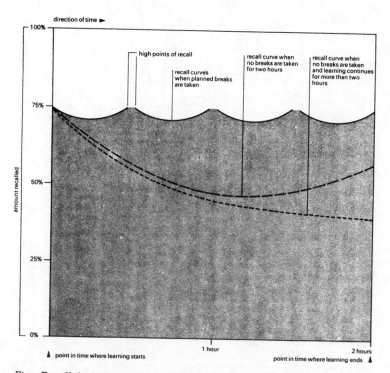

Fig 19 **Recall during learning – with and without breaks. A learning period of between 20–40 minutes produces the best relationship between understanding and recall.** *See text pages 53 and 54.*

Breaks are additionally useful as relaxation points. They get rid of the muscular and mental tension which inevitably builds up during periods of concentration.

Fig 20 **Recall after a learning period – people's estimates.** Graph showing the different kinds of answers people gave when asked to show how their recall functioned after a period of learning. *See text on opposite page.*

Recall after a learning period – discussion of Test 3 and answers

In Test 3 you were asked to fill in a graph indicating the way you thought your recall functioned after a period of learning had been completed. The examples on pages 47 and 48 were answers many people have given when asked this question, although a much wider variety of responses overall was registered.

Apart from those graphed on pages 47 and 48 – other answers included: straight lines plunging almost immediately to nothing: variations on the more rapid drop, some falling to 0%, others always maintaining some per cent, however small; variations on the slower fall-off, also with some falling to 0% and others maintaining; and variations on these themes, showing rises and falls of varying degree. *See fig 20.*

The surprising truth of the matter is that none of the examples shown earlier, and none of the estimates shown, are correct.

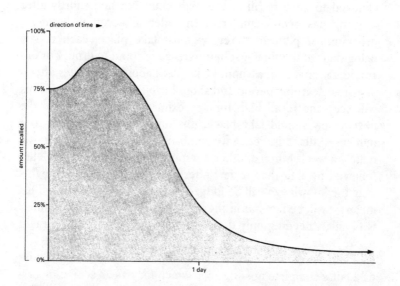

Fig 21 **Graph showing how human recall rises for a short while after learning, and then falls steeply (80% of detail forgotten within 24 hours).** *See text page 58.*

They have all neglected a particularly significant factor: recall after a learning period initially *rises*, and only then declines, following a steeply falling concave curve that levels off and never quite touches the bottom of the graph. *See fig 21.*

Once it is realised that this brief rise does take place, the reason for it can be understood: at the very moment when a learning period is finished, the brain has not had enough time to integrate the new information it has assimilated, especially the last items. It needs a few minutes to complete and link firmly all the interconnections within the new material – to let it 'sink-in'.

The decline that takes place after the small rise is a steep one – within 24 hours of a one-hour learning period at least 80 per cent of detailed information is lost. This enormous drop in the amount remembered must be prevented, and can be by proper techniques of review.

Memory – review

If review is organised properly, the graph shown in fig 19 can be changed to keep recall at the high point reached shortly after learning has been completed. In order to accomplish this, a programmed pattern of review must take place, each review being done at the time just before recall is about to drop. For example, the first review should take place about 10 minutes after a one-hour learning period and should itself take 10 minutes. This will keep the recall high for approximately one day, when the next review should take place, this time for a period of 2 to 4 minutes. After this, recall will probably be retained for approximately a week, when another 2 minute review can be completed followed by a further review after about one month. After this time the knowledge will be lodged in Long Term Memory. This means it will be familiar in the way a personal telephone number is familiar, needing only the most occasional nudge to maintain it. *See fig 22.*

The first review, especially if notes have been taken, should be a fairly complete note revision which may mean scrapping original notes and substituting for them revised and final copy. The second, third and fourth etc. review sessions should take the following form: without referring to final notes, jot down on a piece

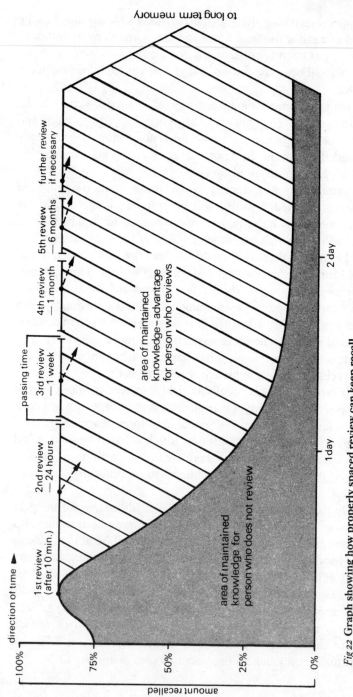

Fig 22 **Graph showing how properly spaced review can keep recall constantly high.** *See text on opposite page.*

of paper everything that can be recalled. This should then be checked against the final notes and any corrections or additions to what has been recalled should be made. Both notes and jottings should be in the form of Mind Maps as explained on pages 112–114.

One of the most significant aspects of proper review is the accumulative effect it has on all aspects of learning, thinking and remembering. The person who does not review is continually wasting the effort he does put in to any learning task, and putting himself at a serious disadvantage.

Each time he approaches a new learning situation his recall of previous knowledge gained will be at a very low ebb, and the connections which should be made automatically will be missed. This will mean that his understanding of the new material will not be as complete as it could be, and that his efficiency and speed through the new material will also be less. This continuingly negative process results in a downward spiral that ends in a general despair of ever being able to learn anything – each time new material is learned it is forgotten, and each time new material is approached it seems to become more oppressive. The result is that many people, after having finished their formal exams, seldom, if ever, approach text books again.

Failure to review is equally as bad for general memory. If each new piece of information is neglected, it will not remain at a conscious level, and will not be available to form new memory connections. As memory is a process which is based on linking and association, the fewer items there are in the 'recall store', the less will be the possibility for new items to be registered and connected.

On the opposite side of this coin, the advantages for the person who *does* review are enormous. The more he maintains his current body of knowledge, the more he will be able to absorb and handle. When he studies, the expanding amount of knowledge at his command will enable him to digest new knowlege far more easily, each new piece of information being absorbed in the context of his existing store of relevant information *see fig 22*. The process is much like that of the traditional snowball rolling, where the snowball gets rapidly bigger the more it rolls and eventually continues rolling under its own momentum.

Review, mental ability and age

The way in which a person reviews has an interesting connection with popular ideas about the way human mental ability declines with age. It is normally assumed that IQ scores, recall ability, ability to see spacial relationships, perceptual speed, speed of judgement, induction, figural relations, associative memory, intellectual level, intellectual speed, semantic relations, formal reasoning and general reasoning etc., decline after reaching a peak at the age of 18 to 25 *see fig 23*. Valid as the figures produced may be, two important factors must be noted:

1 The decline over the life-time is little more than 5 to 10 per cent. When considered in relation to the brain's enormous inherent capacity, this is insignificant.

2 The people who took part in the experiments which arrived at these discouraging figures had been educated traditionally,

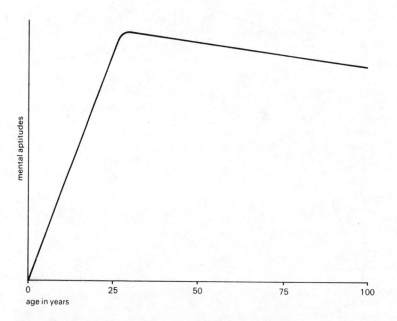

Fig 23 Graph showing standard results of measuring mental aptitudes as a person gets older. It is assumed that after reaching a peak at approximately 18–25, decline is thereafter slow but steady. *See text this page.*

and therefore in most cases would not have been practising proper learning, reviewing and remembering techniques.

Looking at figure 23 it can be easily seen that such a person's mental 'conditioning' would have been at a very low level for an increasing number of years. In other words his real intellectual capacities would have been in 'cold storage'. It is not surprising that such an unused mind would do slightly worse after 20 to 40 years of mis- or no use – it is surprising that it still manages to do as well as it does!

If, on the other hand, the mind were continually used, and its capacities expanded, the effect on the graph for age would be dramatic. This can be seen by taking note of those older people

Memory

mental aptitudes

0   25   50   75   100

age in years

Fig 24 **Graphs such as shown if fig 23 are based on statistics from people taught traditionally. A human being would naturally tend to improve these capacities with age if taught in a manner that complemented and nourished the brain's natural functioning.**

who have remained active and explorative rather than assuming that they were going to get worse as the years passed. Very often their recall is almost total, and their ability to understand and learn new areas of knowledge far surpasses that of equally enthusiastic but younger and less experienced minds.

In studying human mental performance it has been mistakenly assumed that the decline found with age is 'natural' and unavoidable. Instead a closer look should be taken at the people being studied, and then experiments should be performed to find out how abilities can be maximised rather than minimised.

Special memory systems – mnemonics (Test 4)

Since the time of the Greeks certain individuals have impressed their fellow men with the most amazing feats of memory. They have been able to remember: hundreds of items backwards and forwards and in any order; dates and numbers; names and faces; and have been able to perform special memory feats such as memorising whole areas of knowledge perfectly, or remembering decks of cards in the order anyone chose to present them.

In most cases these individuals were using special memorising techniques known as mnemonics. Traditionally these techniques have been scorned as mere tricks, but recently the attitude towards them has begun to change. It has been realised that the methods which initially enable minds to remember something more easily and quickly, and then to remember it for much longer afterwards, must be more than simple tricks.

Current knowledge about the ways in which our minds work shows that these techniques are indeed closely connected to the basic ways in which the brain functions. The use of mnemonic techniques has consequently gained respectability and popularity, and they are currently being taught in universities and schools as additional aids in the general learning process. The improvement of memory performances that can be achieved is quite remarkable, and the range of techniques is wide.

There is not enough space in the present chapter to give a complete coverage, but I shall introduce here the basic theory behind the system, and a simple system for remembering up to ten items.

Let us assume that the items to be remembered are:

1 table
2 feather
3 cat
4 leaf
5 student
6 orange
7 car
8 pencil
9 shirt
10 poker

In order to remember these it is necessary to have some system which enables us to use the associative and linking power of memory to connect them with their proper number.

The best system for this is the Number-Rhyme System, in which each number has a rhyming word connected to it.

The rhyming key words are:

1 bun
2 shoe
3 tree
4 door
5 hive
6 sticks
7 heaven
8 gate
9 vine
10 hen

In order to remember the first list of arbitary words it is necessary to link them in some strong manner with the rhyming words connected to the numbers. If this is done successfully, the answer to a question such as 'what word was connected to number 5?' will be easy. The rhyming word for 5, 'hive', will be recalled automatically and with it will come the connected image of the word that has to be remembered. The numbers, rhyming words, and items to be remembered can be thought of respectively as the clothes rail, the hangers, and the clothes in a clothes cupboard. *See fig 25.*

The important thing in this and all other memory systems is to make sure that the rhyming word and the word to be remembered are totally and securely linked together. In order to do this, the connecting images must be one or many of the following:

exaggerated

The image must be made exceptionally or grotesquely large, or loud, etc.

absurd

Where possible the linked images should form a new image which is humorous or ridiculous.

sexual

If sex can be brought in in anyway, bring it in!

vulgar

Things which are obscene are recalled exceptionally well also!

sensual

As with sex, any of the basic bodily senses will help to form a memorable image.

moving

A moving image usually lasts longer than a static one.

coloured

Coloured as brightly and gaudily as possible.

imaginative

Imaginative in any other way not yet mentioned.

pure

The two items must be linked together with as few other items as possible. Linkages which are too witty, abstract or confused will not help.

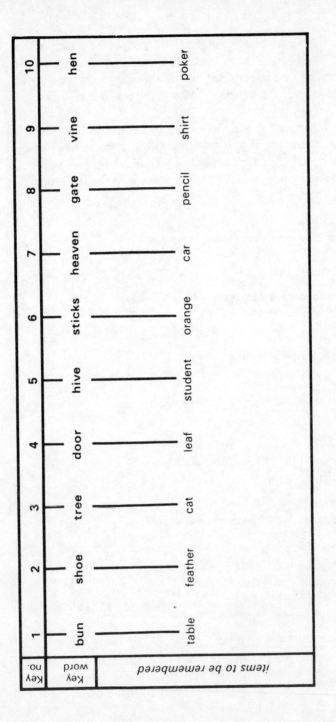

Key no.	1	2	3	4	5	6	7	8	9	10
Key word	bun	shoe	tree	door	hive	sticks	heaven	gate	vine	hen
items to be remembered	table	feather	cat	leaf	student	orange	car	pencil	shirt	poker

Fig 25 The number-rhyme memory system represented as a clothes cupboard. *See text pages 64 and 65.*

It is important, when forming the images, to have a very clear mental picture in front of your inner eye. To achieve this it is often best to close your eyes and to project the image on to the inside of your eyelid.

To make all this clearer, let us try the ten items given.

1 **bun** table

Imagine a giant bun on top of a fragile table which is in the process of crumbling from the weight.

2 **shoe** feather

Imagine your favourite shoe with an enormous feather growing out of the inside, preventing you from putting your shoe on.

3 **tree** cat

Imagine a large tree with either your own cat or a cat you know stuck in the very top branches frantically scrambling about and mewing loudly.

4 **door** leaf

Imagine your bedroom door as one giant leaf.

5 **hive** student

Imagine a student at his desk, and instead of a book in front of him, imagine an enormous bee hive with bees circling it and occasionally attacking him.

6 **sticks** orange

Imagine large sticks puncturing the juicy surface of an orange that is as big as a beach ball.

7 **heaven** car

Imagine all the angels sitting on cars rather than clouds.

8 **gate** pencil

Imagine a gate made completely out of giant pencils rather than normal wood.

9 **vine** shirt

Imagine a vine as large as Jack in the Bean Stalk's bean stalk, and instead of leaves on the vine, hang it all over with brightly coloured shirts blowing in the wind.

10 **hen** poker

Be vulgar!

Now fill in as many of the words as you can on the facing page.

With a little practice it would be possible to remember ten out of ten each time, even though using the same system. The words to be remembered can, like the clothes they were compared to, be taken off the hook and other clothes substituted. The words which must remain constant and which in any case are almost impossible to forget are the rhyming key words.

As mentioned earlier there are many other systems which are equally as easy to remember as this simple one but would take (and already have done) another book to explain. Ones which are particularly useful include the Major System, which enables recall of more than a thousand items in the manner of the Number-Rhyme System, as well as giving a key for memorising numbers and dates, and the Face-Name System which helps prevent the embarrassing and wide-spread habit of not being able to recall either the names or faces of people you have met.

Key words and concepts in remembering

As you will have gathered throughout the development of this chapter, memory is primarily an associative and linking process which depends in large part on key words and key concepts properly imagined.

Although the chapter entitled Memory is coming to an end the next three chapters on Key words and Creative pattern linkages are themselves very closely connected with remembering and recalling. The information in this chapter should be reconsidered after the following chapters have been completed.

In the spaces opposite write the rhyming key word for the Number-Rhyme System, and next to it the words used earlier in the chapter to illustrate the system.

Rhyming key words   word connected

1 _____   _____

2 _____   _____

3 _____   _____

4 _____   _____

5 _____   _____

6 _____   _____

7 _____   _____

8 _____   _____

9 _____   _____

10 _____   _____

Personal Notes

4.
Noting

A: Key words

Overview

- Exercise key words; standard responses
- Key words and concepts – creative and recall
- Memory – a comparison between
  standard note and
  key word noting
- Transition from advanced key word
  note taking to advanced Mind Map
  key word note taking

Exercise and discussion

Imagine that your hobby is reading short stories, that you read at least five a day, and that you keep notes so that you will not forget any of them. Imagine also that in order to ensure a proper recall of each story you use a card filing system. For each story you have one card for the title and author, and a card for every paragraph. On each of these paragraph cards you enter a main and a secondary key word or phrase. The key words/phrases you take either directly from the story or make up yourself because they summarise particularly well.

Imagine further that your ten thousandth story is *Kusa-Hibari* by Lafcadio Hearne, and that you have prepared the title-and-author card.

Now read the story on page 73, and for the purpose of this exercise enter a key recall word or phrase for both the main and secondary idea for the first five paragraphs only, in the space provided on page 76.

Kusa-Hibari   *Lafcadio Hearne*

His cage is exactly two Japanese inches high and one inch and a
half wide: its tiny wooden door, turning upon a pivot, will
scarcely admit the tip of my little finger. But he has plenty of
room in that cage – room to walk, and jump, and fly, for he is so
small that you must look very carefully through the brown-gauze
sides of it in order to catch a glimpse of him. I have always to
turn the cage round and round, several times, in a good light,
before I can discover his whereabouts, and then I usually find
him resting in one of the upper corners – clinging, upside down,
to his ceiling of gauze.

Imagine a cricket about the size of an ordinary mosquito –
with a pair of antennae much longer than his own body, and so
fine that you can distinguish them only against the light.
Kusa-Hibari, or 'Grass-Lark' is the Japanese name of him; and
he is worth in the market exactly twelve cents: that is to say, very
much more than his weight in gold. Twelve cents for such a
gnat-like thing! . . . By day he sleeps or meditates, except while
occupied with the slice of fresh egg-plant or cucumber which
must be poked into his cage every morning . . . to keep him clean
and well fed is somewhat troublesome: could you see him, you
would think it absurd to take any pains for the sake of a creature
so ridiculously small.

But always at sunset the infinitesimal soul of him awakens:
then the room begins to fill with a delicate and ghostly music of
indescribable sweetness – a thin, silvery rippling and trilling as of
tiniest electric bells. As the darkness deepens, the sound
becomes sweeter – sometimes swelling till the whole house
seems to vibrate with the elfish resonance – sometimes thinning
down into the faintest imaginable thread of a voice. But loud or
low, it keeps a penetrating quality that is weird . . . All night the
atomy thus sings: he ceases only when the temple bell proclaims
the hour of dawn.

Now this tiny song is a song of love – vague love of the unseen
and unknown. It is quite impossible that he should ever have
seen or known, in this present existence of his. Not even his
ancestors, for many generations back, could have known
anything of the night-life of the fields, or the amorous value of
song.

They were born of eggs hatched in a jar of clay, in the shop of some insect-merchant: and they dwelt thereafter only in cages. But he sings the song of his race as it was sung a myriad years ago, and as faultlessly as if he understood the exact significance of every note. Of course he did not learn the song. It is a song of organic memory – deep, dim memory of other quintillions of lives, when the ghost of him shrilled at night from the dewy grasses of the hills. Then that song brought him love – and death. He has forgotten all about death: but he remembers the love. And therefore he sings now – for the bride that will never come.

So that his longing is unconsciously retrospective: he cries to the dust of the past – he calls to the silence and the gods for the return of time . . . Human lovers do very much the same thing without knowing it. They call their illusion an Ideal: and their Ideal is, after all, a mere shadowing of race-experience, a phantom of organic memory. The living present has very little to do with it . . . . Perhaps this atom also has an ideal, or at least the rudiment of an ideal; but, in any event, the tiny desire must utter its plaint in vain.

The fault is not altogether mine. I had been warned that if the creature were mated, he would cease to sing and would speedily die. But, night after night, the plaintive, sweet, unanswered trilling touched me like a reproach – became at last an obsession, an afflication, a torment of conscience; and I tried to buy a female. It was too late in the season; there were no more kusa-hibari for sale, – either males or females. The insect-merchant laughed and said, 'He ought to have died about the twentieth day of the ninth month.' (It was already the second day of the tenth month.) But the insect-merchant did not know that I have a good stove in my study, and keep the temperature at above 75°F. Wherefore my grass-lark still sings at the close of the eleventh month, and I hope to keep him alive until the Period of Greatest Cold. However, the rest of his generation are probably dead: neither for love nor money could I now find him a mate. And were I to set him free in order that he might make the search for himself, he could not possibly live through a single night, even if fortunate enough to escape by day the multitude of his natural enemies in the garden – ants, centipedes, and ghastly earth-spiders.

Last evening – the twenty-ninth of the eleventh month – an odd feeling came to me as I sat at my desk: a sense of emptiness in the room. Then I became aware that my grass-lark was silent, contrary to his wont. I went to the silent cage, and found him lying dead beside a dried-up lump of egg-plant as gray and hard as a stone. Evidently he had not been fed for three or four days; but only the night before his death he had been singing wonderfully – so that I foolishly imagined him to be more than usually contented. My student, Aki, who loves insects, used to feed him; but Aki had gone into the country for a week's holiday, and the duty of caring for the grass-lark had developed upon Hana, the housemaid. She is not sympathetic, Hana the housemaid. She says that she did not forget the mite – but there was no more egg-plant. And she had never thought of substituting a slice of onion or of cucumber! . . . I spoke words of reproof to Hana the housemaid, and she dutifully expressed contrition. But the fairy-music had stopped: and the stillness reproaches; and the room is cold, in spite of the stove.

Absurd! . . . I have made a good girl unhappy because of an insect half the size of a barley-grain! The quenching of that infinitesimal life troubled me more than I could have believed possible . . . . Of course, the mere habit of thinking about a creature's wants – even the wants of a cricket – may create, by insensible degrees, an imaginative interest, an attachment of which one becomes conscious only when the relation is broken. Besides, I had felt so much, in the hush of the night, the charm of the delicate voice – telling of one minute existence dependent upon my will and selfish pleasure, as upon the favour of a god – telling me also that the atom of ghost in the tiny cage, and the atom of ghost within myself, were forever but one and the same in the deeps of the Vast of being . . . . And then to think of the little creature hungering and thirsting, night after night and day after day, while the thoughts of his guardian deity were turned to the weaving of dreams! . . . How bravely, nevertheless, he sang on to the very end – an atrocious end, for he had eaten his own legs! . . . May the gods forgive us all – especially Hana the housemaid!

Yet, after all, to devour one's own legs for hunger is not the worst that can happen to a being cursed with the gift of song. There are human crickets who must eat their own hearts in order to sing.

Key words or phrases for main and secondary ideas from Kusa-Hibari

	main	secondary
paragraph 1	_____	_____
paragraph 2	_____	_____
paragraph 3	_____	_____
paragraph 4	_____	_____
paragraph 5	_____	_____

Below you will find sample key words and phrases from the notes of students who have previously done this exercise. Briefly compare and contrast these with your own ideas.

Students' suggested key words and phrases

	main	secondary
paragraph 1	his cage	two Japanese inches
	wooden door	wooden floor
	ceiling of gauze	plenty of room
	small insect	discover whereabouts

paragraph 2	cricket	Grass-Lark
	weight in gold	twelve cents
	antennae	market
	Kusa-Hibari	gnatlike
paragraph 3	sleep	fresh cucumber
	clean and well fed	pains
	occupied	meditation
	absurd	small
paragraph 4	penetrating	silvery rippling
	music	house vibrating
	electric bells	penetrating
	soul	hour of dawn
paragraph 5	Love	night life
	amorous	insect merchant
	the hills	significance
	Death	love and death

In class situations instructors then circled one word from each section:

	main	secondary
paragraph 1	wooden door	discover whereabouts
1	weight in gold	market
3	occupied	pains
4	penetrating	hour of dawn
5	love	night-life

Students were then asked to explain why, in the context of the exercise, these words and phrases and not others had been selected. Answers usually included the following: 'good image words', 'imaginative', 'descriptive', 'appropriate', 'good for remembering', and 'evocative', etc.

Only one student in fifty realised why the instructors had chosen these words: in the context of the exercise the series chosen was disastrous.

To understand why, it is necessary to imagine a time some years after the story has been read when you are going to look at the notes again for recall purposes. Imagine that some friends have played a prank, taking out the title cards of some of your stories and challenging you to remember the titles and authors. You would have no idea to start with to which story your cards referred, and would have to rely solely on them to give you back the correct images.

With the key words at the bottom of page 77, you would probably be forced to link them in the following way: 'wooden door', a general phrase, would gain a mystery-story air when you read 'discover whereabouts'. The next two keys 'weight in gold' and 'market' would confirm this, adding a further touch of intrigue suggesting a criminal activity. The next three key words, 'occupied' 'pains' and 'penetrating' might lead you to assume that one of the characters, perhaps the hero, was personally in difficulty, adding further tension to the ongoing plot as the 'hour of dawn', obviously an important and suspense-filled moment in the story, approached. The final two keys, 'love' and 'night-life' would add a romantic or risqué touch to the whole affair, encouraging you to thumb quickly through the remaining key words in search of further adventures and climaxes! You would have created an interesting new story, but would not remember the original one.

Words which seemed quite good at the time have not, for some reason, proved adequate for recall. To explain why, it is necessary to discuss the difference between key recall words and key creative words, and the way in which they interact after a period of time has passed.

A key recall word or phrase is one which funnels into itself a wide range of special images, and which, when it is triggered, funnels back the same images. It will tend to be a strong noun or verb, on occasion being surrounded by additional key adjectives or adverbs. *See fig 26*.

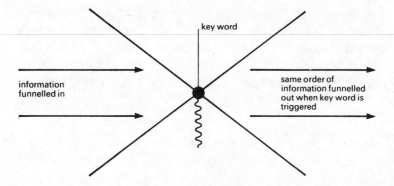

Fig 26 **Diagram representing key recall word.** *See text on opposite page.*

A creative word is one which is particularly evocative and image-forming, but which is far more general than the more directed key recall word. Words like 'ooze' and 'bizarre' are especially evocative but do not necessarily bring back a specific image. *See fig 27.*

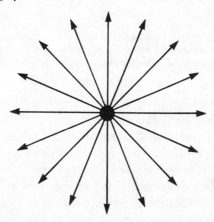

Fig 27 **A creative word sprays out associations in all directions.** *See text this page.*

Apart from understanding the difference between creative and recall words, it is also necessary to understand the nature of words themselves as well as the nature of the brain which uses them.

Every word is 'multi-ordinate', which simply means that each word is like a little centre on which there are many, many little hooks. Each hook can attach to other words to give both words in the new pair slightly different meanings. For example the word 'run' can be hooked quite differently in 'run like hell' and 'her stocking has a run in it'.

Fig 28 **Each word is multi-ordinate, meaning that it has a large number of 'hooks'. Each hook, when it attaches to another word, changes the meaning of the word. Think, for example, of how the word 'run' changes in different phrase contexts.** *See text pages 79 and 80*

In addition to the multi-ordinate nature of words, each brain is also different from each other brain. As shown in the first chapter, the number of connections a brain can make within itself is almost limitless. Each individual also experiences a very different life from each other individual (even if two people are enjoying the 'same experience' together they are in very different worlds: A is enjoying the experience with B as a major part of it, and B is enjoying the experience with A as a major part of it). Similarly the associations that each person will have for any word will be different from everybody else's. Even a simple word like 'leaf' will produce a different series of images for each person who reads or hears it. A person whose favourite colour is green might imagine the general greenness of leaves; someone whose favourite colour is brown, the beauty of autumn; a person who had been injured falling out of a tree, the feeling of fear; a gardener, the different emotions connected with the pleasure of seeing leaves grow and the thought of having to rake them all up when they had fallen, etc. One could go on for ever and still not satisfy the range of associations that you who are reading this book might have when *you* think of leaves.

As well as the unique way in which the mind sees its personal images, each brain is also, by nature, both creative and sense-organising. It will tend to 'tell itself interesting and entertaining stories' as it does for example when we day- or night-dream.

The reason for the failure of the recall and creative words selected from *Kusa-Hibari* can now clearly be seen. When each of the multi-ordinate words or phrases was approached, the mind automatically picked the connecting hooks which were most obvious, most image-producing, or the most sense-making. The mind was consequently led down a path that was more creative than recall based, and a story was constructed that was interesting, but hardly useful for remembering.

Fig 29 **Showing how mind can follow the 'wrong connections' in a series of key words.** *See text this page.*

Key recall words would have forced the mind to make the proper links in the right direction, enabling it to recreate the story even if for all other intentional purposes it had been forgotten.

Fig 30 **Direction of correct associations when proper recall key words have been used.** *See text this page.*

Key versus standard notes

The main body of a person's recalling is of this key concept nature. It is not, as is often assumed, a word-for-word verbatim process. When people describe books they have read or places they have been to, they do not start to 're-read' from memory. They give key concept overviews outlining the main characters, settings, events and add descriptive detail. Similarly the single key word or phrase will bring back whole ranges of experience and sensation. Think for example of the range of images that enter your mind when you read the word 'child'.

How, then, does acceptance of these facts about key recall affect our attitude toward the structure of note taking?

Because we have become so used to speaking and writing words, we have mistakenly assumed that normal sentence structure is the best way to remember verbal images and ideas. Thus the majority of students and even graduates have taken notes in a normal literary fashion similar to the example of a university student whose notes were rated 'good' by his professor. *See facing page.*

Our new knowledge of key concepts and recall has shown that in this type of notes 90 per cent of the words are not necessary for recall purposes. This frighteningly high figure becomes even more frightening when a closer look is taken at what happens with standard sentence notes:

1. Time is wasted recording words which have no bearing on memory (estimated waste – 90%).

2. Time is wasted re-reading the same unnecessary words (estimated waste – 90%).

3. Time is wasted searching for the words which *are* key, for they are usually not distinguished by any marks and thus blend in with other non-recall words.

4. The connections between key words are interrupted by words that separate them. We know that memory works by association and any interference by non recall words will make the connections less strong.

5. The key words are separated in time by intervening words: after one key word or phrase has been read it will take at least

Fig 31 **An example of traditionally 'good' university student's notes.**
See text on opposite page.

a few seconds to get to the next. The longer the time between connections, the less chance there will be of proper connection being made.

6 The key words are separated in space by their distance from each other on the page. As with the point made about time, the greater the distance between the words, the less chance of there being a proper connection.

You are advised to practise key word and phrase selection from any previous notes made during periods of study. It will also be helpful at this point for you to summarise this chapter in key note form.

In addition, reconsider key and creative words in the light of the information in the chapter on Memory, especially the section dealing with mnemonic techniques. Similarly the memory chapter itself can be reconsidered in the light of this chapter, with a similar emphasis on the relationship and similarities between mnemonic systems and key and creative concepts.

The review graph is another important consideration. Review is made much easier when notes are in key form, because less time is expended, and because the recall itself will be superior and more complete. Any weak linkages will also be cemented more firmly in the early stages.

Finally, linkages between key words and concepts should always be emphasised and where possible simple lists and lines of key words should be avoided. In the following chapter advanced methods of key word linking and patterning will be explained in full.

Personal Notes

B: Mind maps for recall and creative thinking

Overview

- Exercise
- Linear history of speech and print
- Contrast: the structure of the brain
- Advanced note taking and mapping techniques

Exercise

In the space below, and starting immediately after having reached the end of this paragraph, prepare a half-hour speech on the topic of Space Travel. Allow no more than five minutes for the task, whether or not you have finished. This exercise will be referred to later in the chapter, before which time the problems experienced in performing the task should also be noted here or in a notebook.

Space travel notes

Problems experienced

Linear history of speech and print

For the last few hundred years it has been popularly thought that man's mind worked in a linear or list-like manner. This belief was held primarily because of the increasing reliance on our two main methods of communication, speech and print.

In speech we are restricted, by the nature of time and space, to speaking and hearing one word at a time. Speech was thus seen as a linear or line-like process between people. *See fig 32.*

Fig 32 **Speech has traditionally been seen as a list-like affair.** *See text page 87.*

Print was seen as even more linear. Not only was the individual forced to take in units of print in consecutive order, but print was laid out on the page in a series of lines or rows.

This linear emphasis overflowed into normal writing or notetaking procedures. Virtually everyone was (and still is) trained in school to take notes in sentences or vertical lists. (Most readers will probably have prepared their half-hour speech in one of these two ways, as shown in fig33). The acceptance of this way of thinking is so long-standing that little has been done to contradict it.

However, recent evidence shows the brain to be far more multi-dimensional and pattern making, suggesting that in the speech/print arguments there must be fundamental flaws.

The argument which says that the brain functions linearly because of the speech patterns it has evolved fails to consider, as do the supporters for the absolute nature of IQ tests, the nature of the organism. It is easy to point out that when words travel from one person to another they necessarily do so in a line, but this is not really the point. More to the point is, the question: 'How does the brain which is speaking, and the brain which is receiving the words, deal with them *internally*?

The answer is that the brain is most certainly *not* dealing with them in simple lists and lines. You can verify this by thinking of the way in which your own thought processes work while you are speaking to someone else. You will observe that although a single line of words is coming out, a continuing and enormously complex process of sorting and selecting is taking place in your

A Normal line structure – sentenced-based

B Standard list structure – order-of-importance-based

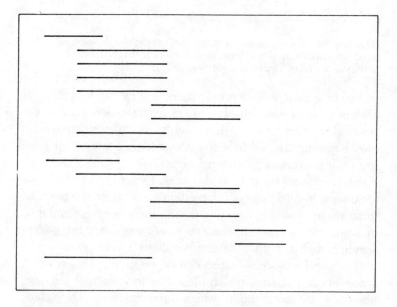

Fig 33 **Standard forms of 'good' or 'neat' notes.**

mind throughout the conversation. Whole networks of words and ideas are being juggled and interlinked in order to communicate a certain meaning to the listener.

Similarly the listener is not simply observing a long list of words like someone sucking up spaghetti. He is receiving each word in the context of the words that surround it. At the same time he is also giving the multi-ordinate nature of each word his own special interpretation as dictated by the structure of his personal information patterns and will be analysing, coding and criticising throughout the process.

Fig 34 **It is the network inside the mind, and not the simple order of word presentation, which is more important to an understanding of the way we relate to words.** *See text pages 88–90.*

You may have noticed people suddenly reacting to words you liked or thought were harmless. They react this way because the associations they have for these words are different from your own. Knowing this will help you to understand more clearly the nature of conversations, disagreements and misunderstandings.

The argument for print is also weak. Despite the fact that we are trained to read units of information one after each other, that these are presented in lines and that we therefore write and note in lines, such linear presentation is not necessary for understanding, and in many instances is a disadvantage.

The mind is perfectly capable of taking in information which is non-linear. In its day-to-day life it does this nearly all the time, observing all those things which surround it which include common *non*-linear forms of print: photographs, illustration, diagrams, etc. It is only our society's enormous reliance on linear information which has obscured the issue.

The brain's non-linear character is further confirmed by recent biochemical physiological and psychological research. Each area of research is discovering that the organism is not only non-linear but is so complex and interlinked as to defy any final description.

The brain and advanced noting

If the brain is to relate to information most efficiently the information must be structured in such a way as to 'slot in' as easily as possible. It follows that if the brain works primarily with key concepts in an interlinked and integrated manner, our notes and our word relations should in many instances be structured in this way rather than in traditional 'lines'.

Rather than starting from the top and working down in sentences or lists, one should start from the centre or main idea and branch out as dictated by the individual ideas and general form of the central theme.

Fig 35 **Initial ideas jotted around a centre.** *See text this page.*

A mind map such as that outlined in fig 35 has a number of advantages over the linear form of note taking.

1 The centre or main idea is more clearly defined.
2 The relative importance of each idea is clearly indicated.

More important ideas will be nearer the centre and less important ideas will be near the edge.

3 The links between the key concepts will be immediately recognisable because of their proximity and connection.

4 As a result of the above, recall and review will be both more effective and more rapid.

5 The nature of the structure allows for the easy addition of new information without messy scratching out or squeezing in, etc.

6 Each map made will look and be different from each other map. This will aid recall.

7 In the more creative areas of note making such as essay preparations etc, the open-ended nature of the map will enable the brain to make new connections far more readily.

In connection with these points, and especially with the last one, you should now do an exercise similar to your space travel speech notes at the beginning of this chapter, but this time using a mind map rather than the more linear methods.

In the space provided on page 94 branch out in the manner indicated in figure 35 in preparation for a speech on 'Myself'.

While doing this exercise a number of things should be noted.

1 Words should be printed in capitals. For reading-back purposes a printed map gives a more photographic, more immediate, and more comprehensive feed-back. The little extra time that it takes to print is amply made up for in the time saved when reading back.

2 The printed words should be on lines, and each line should be connected to other lines. This is to guarantee that the mind map has basic structure.

3 Words should be in 'units', i.e. one word per line. This leaves each word more free hooks and gives note-taking more freedom and flexibility

4 In creative efforts of this nature the mind should be left as 'free' as possible. Any 'thinking' about where things should go or whether they should be included will simply slow down the

process. The idea is to recall everything your mind thinks of around the central idea. As your mind will generate ideas faster than you can write, there should be almost no pause – if you do pause you will probably notice your pen or pencil dithering over the page. The moment you notice this get it back down and carry on. Do not worry about order or organisation as this will in many cases take care of itself. If it does not, a final ordering can be completed at the end of the exercise.

Start the exercise now.

Although this first attempt at mapping may have been a little difficult, you will probably have noticed that the experience is quite different from that of the first exercise, and that the problems too may have been quite different.

Problems often noted in the first exercise include;

order	organisation
logical sequence	time distribution
beginning	emphasis of ideas
ending	mental blocking

These problems arise because people are attempting to select the main headings and ideas one after the other, and are attempting to put them into order as they go – they are trying to order a structure of speech without having considered all the information available. This will inevitably lead to confusion and the problems noted, for new information which turns up after the first few items might suddenly alter the whole outlook on the subject. With a linear approach this type of happening is disruptive, but with the map approach it is simply part of the overall process, and can be handled properly.

Another disadvantage of the list-like method is that it operates against the way in which the brain works. Each time an idea is thought of it is put on the list and forgotten while a new idea is searched for. This means that all the multi-ordinate and associative possibilities of each word are cut off and boxed away while the mind wanders around in search of another new idea.

Myself

With the map approach each idea is left as a totally open possibility, so that the map grows organically and increasingly, rather than being stifled.

You might find it interesting to compare your efforts so far with the efforts of three school children. *See figs 36 to 38.*

Figure 36, page 102 shows the normal writing of a fourteen-year-old boy who was described as reasonably bright, but messy, confused, and mentally disorganised. The example of his linear writing represents his 'best notes' and explains clearly why he was described as he was. The mind map of English which he completed in five minutes shows almost completely the reverse, suggesting that we can often misjudge a child by the method in which we require him to express himself.

Figure 37, page 103 is the mind map of a boy who twice failed O level Economics and who was described by the teacher as having enormous thinking and learning problems combined with an almost total lack of knowledge of his subject. The map which also was completed in five minutes, shows quite the reverse.

Figure 38, page 104 is a mind map done by an A Level grammar school girl on pure Mathematics. When this map was shown to a Professor of Mathematics he estimated that it was done by a University Honours student and that it probably took two days to complete. In fact it took the girl only twenty minutes. The map enabled her to display an extraordinary creativity in a subject which is normally considered dry, dull and oppressive. It could have been even better if each line had contained only 'units' of words instead of phrases. Her use of form and shape to augment the words will give an indication of the diversity possible in these structures. The following chapter extends this idea.

The mind maps on pages 97–100 represent a new method for noting.

There are four of them, and they summarise the first four chapters of the book.

A fifth page has been left blank for you to create a mind map of Chapter 5 for yourself.

In these mind maps key words and images are linked to each other around a main centre (in these cases, the overall theme of a chapter), and a mental picture is built up of an entire thought structure.

- The theory and method for making these patterned notes is fully outlined in sections B and C of chapter 4, starting on page 86.

- Use the notes for each chapter as a preview of what is to come; they will make the reading of the chapter easier.

- After finishing a chapter, look at its patterns once again. This will serve as a good review, and will help you to remember what you have read.

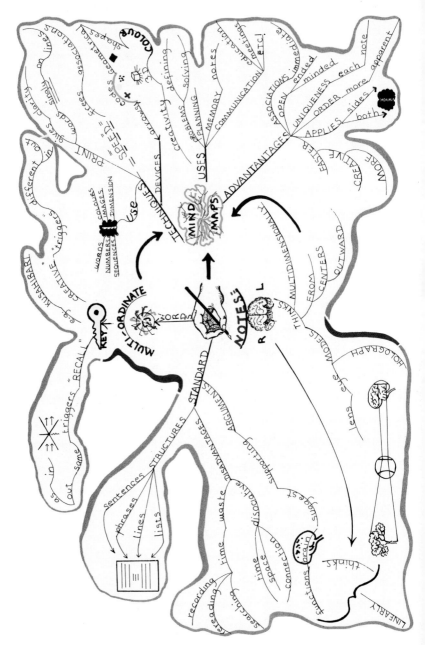

Draw your own mind map of chapter five

7) SETTING   Time + places in which the novel is situated

8) IMAGERY   the Kind of images the author uses to describe (usually by simile or metaphor)

9) SYMBOLISM   One thing stands for another
the witches in Macbeth signifying evil

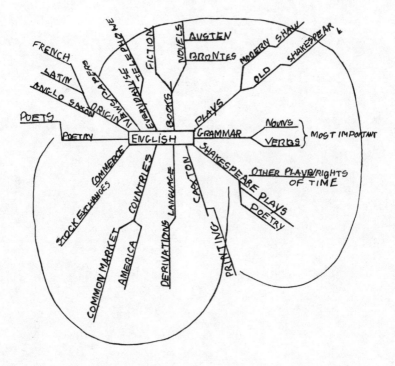

Fig 36 The 'best notes' in linear writing of a 14 year-old boy, and his mind map notes on English. *See text page 95.*

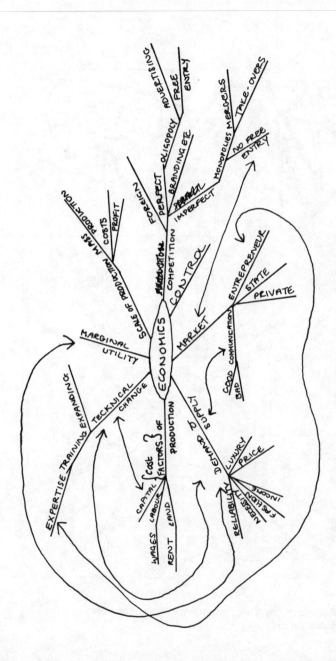

Fig 37 **Mind map by a boy who twice failed O level Economics.** *See text page 95.*

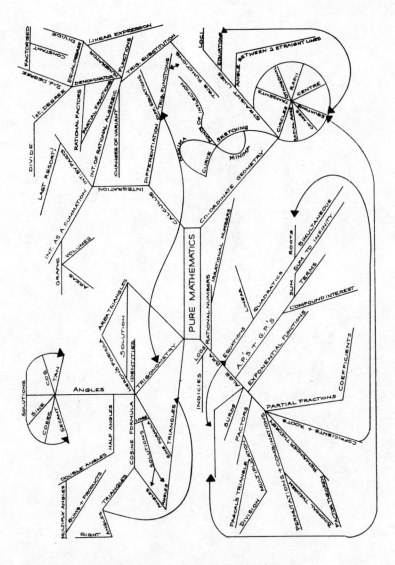

Fig 38 Mind map by an A level grammar school girl on pure
Mathematics. *See text page 95.*

Personal Notes

C: Mind maps – advanced methods and uses

Overview

- Models for the brain
- Technology and new insights into ourselves
- The left and right brain and mind mapping
- Advanced techniques
- Wider application of patterning techniques

Models of perception – brain – mind

As recently as the 1950s the camera provided the model for our perception and mental imaging: the lens of the camera corresponded to the lens of the eye, and the photographic plate to the brain itself. *See fig 39.* This conception was held for some time but was very inadequate. You can confirm this inadequacy by doing the following exercises: in the way that one normally does when drowsily day-dreaming, close your eyes and imagine your favourite object. Having clearly registered the image on your inner eye, perform the following activities.

- Rotate it in front of you
- Look at it from the top
- Look at it from underneath
- Change its colour at least three times
- Move it away as if it were seen from a long distance
- Bring it close again
- Make it gigantic
- Make it tiny
- Totally change the shape of it
- Make it disappear
- Bring it back

These feats can be performed without much difficulty; the apparatus and machinery of a camera could not even begin to perform them.

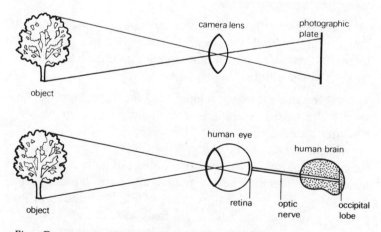

Fig 39 Contrary to earlier thought the brain operates in a much more complex manner than the camera. *See text this page.*

Modern technology

Recent developments in more refined technology have fortunately given us a much better analogy: the hologram.

In this technique, an especially concentrated light or laser beam is split into two. One half of the ray is directed to the plate, while the other half is bounced off the image and then directed back to the other half of the ray. The special holographic plate records the millions of fragments into which the rays shatter when they collide. When this plate is held up in front of laser beams directed at special angles towards it, the original image is recreated. Amazingly, it is not recreated as a flat picture on the plate, but is perfectly duplicated as a three-dimensional ghost object that hangs in space. If the object is looked at from above, below or the side, it is seen in exactly the same way as the original object would be seen.

Even more amazingly, if the original holographic plate is rotated through 90 degrees, as many as 90 images can be recorded on the same plate with no interference.

And to add still further to the extraordinary nature of this new development, if the plate is taken and smashed to smithereens with a hammer, each particle of the shattered plate will, when it is placed in front of the specially direct lasers, still produce the complete three-dimensional ghost.

The holograph thus becomes a far more reasonable model than the camera for the way in which our brain works, and begins to give us some idea of just how complex an organism it is that we carry about with us.

But even this extremely refined piece of technology falls far short of the unique capabilities of the brain. The holograph certainly approximates more closely the three-dimensional nature of our imaginations, but its storage capacity is puny compared to the millions of images that our brains can call up at an instant's notice, and randomly. The holograph is also static. It cannot perform any of the directional exercises of the kind described on pages 107 and 108 which the brain finds so easy and yet which must involve the most unimaginably intricate machinery. And even if the holograph were able to accomplish all this, it would not be able to do what our minds can: to see its own self, with eyes closed, performing the operations!

The above gives considerable cause for thought, and even our most advanced sciences have as yet made little progress in this most interesting area of current research.

Advanced mind maps

Observing that the brain handles information better if the information is designed to 'slot in', and observing also the information from this chapter about the dimensional nature of the mind, it follows that notes which are themselves more 'holographic' and creative will be far more readily understood, appreciated and recalled.

There are many devices we can use to make such notes:

arrows

These can be used to show how concepts which appear on different parts of a pattern are connected. The arrow can be single or multi-headed and can show backward and forward directions.

codes

Asterisks, exclamation marks, crosses and question marks as well as many other indicators can be used next to words to show connections or other 'dimensions'.

geometrical shapes

Squares, oblongs, circles and ellipses etc. . . . . can be used to mark areas or words which are similar in nature – for example triangles might be used to show areas of possible solution in a problem-solving pattern. Geometrical shapes can also be used to show order of importance. Some people, for example, prefer to use a square always for their main centre, oblongs for the ideas near the centre, triangles for ideas of next importance, and so on.

artistic three dimension

Each of the geometrical shapes mentioned, and many others, can be given perspective. For example, making a square into a cube. The ideas printed in these shapes will thus 'stand off' the page.

creativity/images

Creativity can be combined with the use of dimension by making aspects of the pattern fit the topic. One man, for example, when doing a pattern on atomic physics, used the nucleus of an atom and the electrons that surrounded it, as the centre for his pattern.

colour

Colour is particularly useful as a memory and creative aid. It can be used, like arrows, to show how concepts which appear on different parts of the pattern are connected. It can also be used to mark off the boundaries between major areas of a pattern.

VBGYOR

Mind Maps and the Left and Right Brain.

At this point it is useful to consider how recent research into the brain adds strength to the points raised so far. In light of the fact, as already outlined, that the brain handles information better if the information is designed to 'slot in', consider the left and right brain research of Roger Sperry and Robert Ornstein. This research *alone* would lead you to conclude that a note taking and thought-organisation technique designed to satisfy the needs of the whole brain would have to include not only words, numbers, order, sequence, and lines, but *also* colour, images, dimension, symbols, and visual rhythms etc: in other words Mind Maps.

Fig 40 The left and right brain.

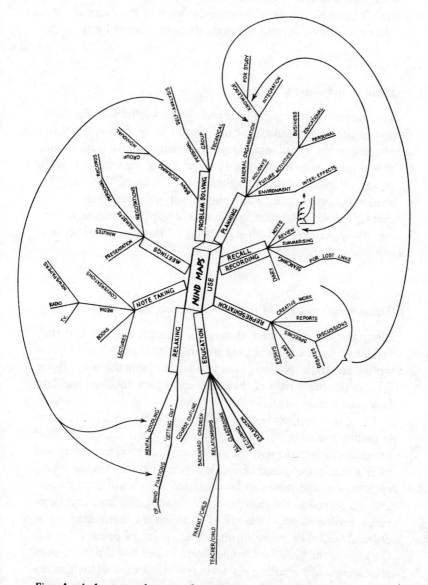

Fig 41 A mind map on the uses of mind maps. *See text page 112.*

From *whatever* perspective one approaches the question, be it from the nature of words and information, the function of recall, holographic models of the brain, or recent brain research, the conclusions in the end are identical – in order to fully utilise the brain's capacity, we need to consider each of the elements that add up to the whole, and integrate them in a unified way.

Mind maps – uses

The nature of mind maps is intimately connected with the function of the mind, and they can be used in nearly every activity where thought, recall, planning or creativity are involved. Figure 41 is a mind map of the use of mind maps, showing this wide variety of uses. Detailed explanation of each of these aspects would of course take up a large book, but in the remainder of this chapter I shall explain the application of maps to the speech writing, essay writing, examination type of task; to meetings and communications, and to note taking.

Transforming a mind map to a speech, article etc.

Many people, when first shown mind maps, assume that they cannot be used for any linear purpose, such as giving a talk or writing an article. Nothing could be further from the truth. If you refer to the mind map of this chapter on page 100, you will find how such a transformation took place:

Once the map has been completed, the required information is readily available. All that is necessary is to decide the final order in which to present the information. A good mind map will offer a number of possibilities. When the choice is being made, each area of the map can be encircled with a different colour, and numbered in the correct order. Putting this into written or verbal form is simply a matter of outlining the major areas to be covered, and then going through them point by point, following the logic of the branched connections. In this way the problem of redrafting and redrafting yet again is eliminated – all the gathering and organising will have been completed at the map stage.

Using these techniques at Oxford University, students were able to complete essays in one third of the previous time while receiving higher marks.

Note taking

It is advisable, when taking notes, to have two blank pages ongoing at the same time. The left-hand page should be for mapped information and the right-hand page for more linear or graphic information such as formulas, special lists, and graphs etc. *See fig 42.*

When taking notes, especially from lectures, it is important to remember that key words and images are essentially all that is

Fig 42 Recommended general form for note taking. Two pages should be used concurrently, one for mind maps, the other for graphic or more linear information. These example notes on body, mind and spirit may originally 'look messy' but they are in fact neater than traditionally 'neat' notes. *See text pages 112 and 114.*

needed. It is also important to remember that the final structure will not become apparent till the end. Any notes made will therefore probably be semi-final rather than final copy. The first few words noted may be fairly disconnected until the theme of the lecture becomes apparent. It is necessary to understand clearly the value of so-called 'messy' as opposed to 'neat' notes, for many people feel apprehension at having a scrawly, arrowed, non-linear page of notes developing in front of them. 'Neat' notes are traditionally those which are organised in an orderly and linear manner. *See fig 33* in the previous chapter. 'Messy' notes are those which are 'untidy' and 'all over the page'. *See fig 42*. The word 'messy' used in this way refers to the *look* and not to the *content*.

In note taking it is primarily the content and not the look that is of importance. The notes which look 'neat' are, in informational terms, messy. As explained on pages 93 and 95, the key information is disguised, disconnected, and cluttered with many informationally irrelevant words. The notes which look 'messy' are informationally far neater. They show immediately the important concepts, the connections, and even in some cases the crossings-out and the objections.

Mapped notes in their final form are usually neat in any case and it seldom takes more than ten minutes to finalise an hour's notes on a fresh sheet of paper. This final map reconstructing is by no means a waste of time, and if the learning period has been organised properly will fit in perfectly as the first review. *See pages 58 to 60*.

Communications and meetings

Meetings, notably those for planning or problem solving, often degenerate into situations where each person listens to the others only in order to make his own point as soon as the previous speaker has finished. In such meetings many excellent points are passed over or forgotten, and much time is wasted. A further aggravation is that points which are finally accepted are not necessarily the best, but are those made by the most vociferous or most important speakers.

These problems can be eliminated if the person who organises the meeting uses a mind map structure. On a board at the front of the room the central theme of the discussion, together with a couple of the sub themes, should be presented in basic map form. The members of the meeting will have preknowledge of what it is about, and will hopefully have come prepared. As each member finishes the point he is making, he can be asked to summarise it in key form, and to indicate where on the overall mind map he thinks his point should be entered.

The following are the advantages of this approach:

1 The contribution of each person is registered and recorded properly.

2 No information is lost.

3 The importance given to ideas will pertain more to what was said than to who said it.

4 Digressions and long wafflings will be eliminated because people will be talking more to the point.

5 After the meeting each individual will have a mapped record and will therefore not have lost most of what is said by the following morning.

One further advantage of mind maps, especially in note taking and communications, is that the individual is kept continually and actively involved in the complete structure of what is going on, rather than being concerned solely with 'getting down' the last point made. This more complete involvement will lead to a much greater critical and analytical facility, a much greater integration, a much greater ability to recall and a much greater overall understanding.

Personal Notes

5.
The Buzan organic study method

The subject of Study is divided into three sections:
Introduction, Preparation, and Application.

A: Introduction

Overview

- Problems of 'getting down' to study
- Reasons for the fear and reluctance many people feel
  when approaching study books
- Problems arising from the use of standard study
  techniques
- New study techniques

Approaching the study situation – a problem before you start

The Six-o'clock-In-The-Evening-Enthusiastic-Determined-And-Well-Intentioned-Studier-Until-Midnight is a person with whom you are probably already familiar. At 6 o'clock he approaches his desk, and carefully organises everything in preparation for the study period to follow. Having everything in place he next carefully adjusts each item again, giving him time to complete the first excuse: he recalls that in the morning he did not have quite enough time to read all items of interest in the newspaper. He also realises that if he is going to study it is best to have such small items completely out of the way before settling down to the task at hand.

He therefore leaves his desk, browses through the newspaper and notices as he browses that there are more articles of interest than he had originally thought. He also notices, as he leafs through the pages, the entertainment section. At this point it will seem like a good idea to plan for the evening's first break – perhaps an interesting half-hour programme between 8 and 8.30 pm.

He finds the programme, and it inevitably starts at about 7 pm.

At this point, he thinks 'well, I've had a difficult day and it's not too long before the programme starts, and I need a rest anyway and the relaxation will really help me to get down to studying. . . .' He returns to his desk at 7.45 pm, because the beginning of the next programme was also a bit more interesting than he thought it would be.

At this stage, he still hovers over his desk tapping his book reassuringly as he remembers that phone call to a friend which, like the articles of interest in the newspapers, is best cleared out of the way before the serious studying begins.

The phone call, of course, is much more interesting and longer than originally planned, but eventually the intrepid studier finds himself back at his desk at about 8.30 pm.

At this point in the proceedings he actually sits down at the desk, opens the book with a display of physical determination, and starts to read (usually page one) as he experiences the first pangs of hunger and thirst. This is disastrous because he realises that the longer he waits to satisfy the pangs, the worse they will get, and the more interrupted his study concentration will be.

The obvious and only solution is a light snack. This, in its preparation, grows like the associative structure of a mind map, as more and more tasty items are linked to the central core of hunger. The snack becomes a feast.

Having removed this final obstacle the desk is returned to with the certain knowledge that this time there is nothing that could possibly interfere with the dedication. The first couple of sentences on page one are looked at again . . . as the studier realises that his stomach is feeling decidedly heavy and a general drowsiness seems to have set in. Far better at this juncture to watch that other interesting half-hour programme at 10 o'clock, after which the digestion will be mostly completed and the rest will enable him to *really* get down to the task at hand.

At 12 o'clock we find him asleep in front of the TV.

Even at this point, when he has been woken up by whoever comes into the room, he will think that things have not gone too badly, for after all he has had a good rest, a good meal, watched some interesting and relaxing programmes, fulfilled his social commitments to his friends, digested the day's information, and got everything completely out of the way so that tomorrow, at 6 o'clock . . . .

The study book is a threat

The above episode is amusing, but the implications of it are significant and serious.

On one level the story is encouraging because, by the very fact that it is a problem experienced by everybody it confirms what has long been suspected: that everyone is creative and inventive, and that the feelings that many have about being uncreative are not necessary. The creativity demonstrated in the example of the reluctant student is not applied very usefully. But the diversity and originality with which we all make up reasons for *not* doing things suggests that each person has a wealth of talent which could be applied in more positive directions!

Fig 43 At the present time information is being given more importance and emphasis than the individual. As a result he is being mentally swamped and almost literally 'weighed down' by it all. Both the information and publication explosions are still continuing at staggering rates, while the ability of the individual to handle and study it all remains neglected. If he is ever to cope with the situation he must learn not more 'hard facts' but new ways of handling and studying the information – new ways of using his natural abilities to learn, think, recall, create, and solve problems. *See also fig 45 and text page 125.*

On another level the story is discouraging because it shows up the wide-spread and underlying fear that most of us experience when confronted with a study text.

This reluctance and fear arises from the examination-based school system in which the child is presented with books on the subjects he is 'taking' at school. He knows that text books are 'harder' than story books and novels; he also knows that they represent a lot of work; and he further knows that he will be tested on his knowledge of the information from the books.

The fact that the type of book is 'hard' is discouraging in itself. The fact that the book represents work is also discouraging, because the child instinctively knows that he is unable to read, note, and remember properly.

And the fact that he is going to be tested is often the most serious of the three difficulties. It is well known that this threat can completely disrupt the brain's ability to work in certain situations. The number of cases are enormous of people who literally cannot write anything in an exam situation despite the fact that they know their subject thoroughly – as are the number of cases of people who, even though they are able to write some form of answer, have gigantic mental blocks where whole areas of knowledge are completely forgotten during an exam period. And in even more extreme cases many people have been known to spend a whole two hour period writing frantically, assuming that they were answering the question, but in fact repeating over and over again either their own name or one word.

Faced with this kind of threat, which for many is truly terrifying, the child has one of two choices: he can either study and face one set of consequences, or not study and face a different set of consequences. If he studies and does badly, then he has proven himself 'incapable', 'unintelligent', 'stupid', a 'dunce' or whatever the appropriate negative expression is at the time. Of course this is not really the case, but he has no way of knowing that it is the system which is not testing him properly, and not his own ineptitude causing the 'failure'.

If he does *not* study, the situation is quite different. Confronted with having failed a test or exam, he can immediately say that of course he failed it because he 'didn't study and wasn't interested in that kind of stuff anyway'.

By doing this, he solves the problem in a number of ways:

1 He avoids both the test and the threat to his self-esteem that studying would involve;
2 He has a perfect excuse for failing;
3 He gets respect from the other children because he is daring to attack a situation which is frightening to them. It is interesting to note that such a child will often find himself in the position of a leader.

It is also interesting to note that even those who do make the decision to study will still reserve a little part of themselves for behaving like the non-studier. The person who gets scores as high as 80 or 90 per cent will also be found using exactly the same excuses for not getting 100 per cent, as the non-studier uses for failing.

Fig 44 In traditional education information is given or 'taught' about the different areas of knowledge that surround the individual. The direction and flow is *from* the subject *to* the individual – he is simply given the information, and is expected to absorb, learn and remember as much as he possibly can. *See also fig 43 and text pages 119–123.*

Old and new study approaches

The situations described above are unsatisfactory for everyone concerned, and have arisen for various reasons, many of them outlined in earlier parts of this book. One further and major reason for poor study results lies in the way we have approached both study techniques and the information we wanted people to study.

We have surrounded the person with a confusing mass of different subjects or 'disciplines' demanding that he learn, remember and understand a frightening array under headings such as Mathematics, Physics, Chemistry, Biology, Zoology, Botany, Anatomy, Physiology, Sociology, Psychology, Anthropology, Philosophy, History, Geography, Trigonometry, Paleontology, etc. In each of these subject areas the individual has been and is still presented with series of dates, theories, facts, names, and general ideas. *See fig 44.* What this really means is that we have been taking a totally lopsided approach to study and to the way in which a person deals with and relates to the information and knowledge that surrounds him. *See figs 44 and 45.*

As can be seen from the figures we are concentrating far too much on information about the 'separate' areas of knowledge. We are also laying too much stress on asking the individual to feed back facts in pre-digested order or in pre-set forms such as standard examination papers or formal essays.

This approach has also been reflected in the standard study techniques recommended in Schools, Universities, Institutes of Further Education and text books. These techniques have been 'grid' approaches in which it is recommended that a series of steps always be worked through on any book being studied. One common suggestion is that any reasonably difficult study book should always be read through three times in order to ensure a complete understanding. This is obviously a very simple example, but even the many more developed approaches tend to be comparatively rigid and inflexible – simply standard systems to be repeated on each studying occasion.

It is obvious that methods such as these cannot be applied with success to every study book. There is an enormous difference between studying a text on Literary Criticism and studying a text on Higher Mathematics. In order to study properly, a technique is needed which does not force the same approach to such different materials.

First, it is necessary to start working from the individual outwards. Rather than bombarding him with books, formulas and examinations we must begin to concentrate on teaching each person how he or she *can* study most efficiently. We must teach

Fig 45 In the new forms of education, the previous emphases must be reversed. Instead of first teaching the individual facts about other things, we must first teach him facts about himself – facts about how he *can* learn, think, recall, create, and solve problems etc. *See text page 125.*

ourselves how our eyes work when we read, how we remember, how we think, how we can learn more effectively, how we can organise noting, how we can solve problems and in general how we can best use our abilities, whatever the subject matter.

One is tempted to note here that in our society we have Instruction Manuals and 'How To Do It' booklets on nearly everything, including the simplest of machines. But when it comes to the most complicated, complex, and important organism of all, ourselves, we offer practically no help.

Most of the problems outlined in the first chapter will be eliminated when we finally do change the emphasis away from the subject toward the individual and how he can select and understand any information he wants to. People will be equipped to study and remember whatever area of knowledge is interesting or necessary. Things will not have to be 'taught to' or 'crammed in'. Each person will be able to range subjects at his own pace, going for help and personal supervision only when he realises it is necessary. *See fig 45.*

Yet another advantage of this approach is that it will make both teaching and learning much easier, more enjoyable and more productive. By concentrating on the individual and his abilities we will finally and sensibly have placed the learning situation in its proper perspective.

Personal Notes

B: Preparation

The Organic Study Method is divided into two main sections: Preparation and Application. Each of these sections is divided into four sub sections:

Preparation   Time
                 Amount
                 Knowledge
                 Questions

Application   Overview
                 Preview
                 Inview
                 Review

It is important to note at the outset that although the main steps are presented in a certain order, this order is by no means essential and can be changed, subtracted from and added to as the study texts warrant.

This section will deal with the Preparation:

Overview

- **The browse**
- **Deciding on the best use of time**
- **Defining the areas of study (amount)**
- **Gathering all the information the reader currently has about the subject**
- **Defining goals and reasons for studying in the first place**

The Browse

Before doing anything else, it is *essential* to 'browse' or look through the entire book or periodical you are about to study. The browse should be done in the way you would look through a book you were considering buying in a bookshop, or in the way you would look through a book you were considering taking out from the library. In other words casually, but rather rapidly, flipping through the pages, getting the general 'feel' of the book, observing the organisation and structure, the level of difficulty, the proportion of diagrams and illustrations to text, the location of any results, summaries and conclusions sections etc. A particularly useful method for browsing is that as outlined in the Chapter on reading more efficiently and faster, Exercise 7b, page 41 – using the visual guide to scan each page at four seconds a page, continuing, not for only one minute, but until the complete book has been surveyed.

Once the browse has been completed, the four major steps of preparation can then be dealt with far more effectively.

Time and amount

These two aspects can be dealt with simultaneously because the theory behind them both is similar.

The first thing to do when sitting down to study a text book is to decide on the period of time to be devoted to it. Having done this, decide what amount to cover in the time allocated.

The reason for insisting on these two initial steps is not arbitrary, and is supported by the findings of the Gestalt Psychologists, and some of the most recent findings in Systems Theory (before reading on, look at figure 46).

The Gestalt Psychologists discovered that the human brain has a very strong tendency to complete things – thus most readers will find that they labelled the shapes in figure 46 straight line, cylinder, square, elipse or oval, zig-zag line, circle, triangle, wavy or curved line, rectangle. In fact the 'circle' is not a circle but a 'broken circle'. Many actually see this broken circle as a circle. Others see it as a broken circle but assume that the artist intended to complete it.

1 _____

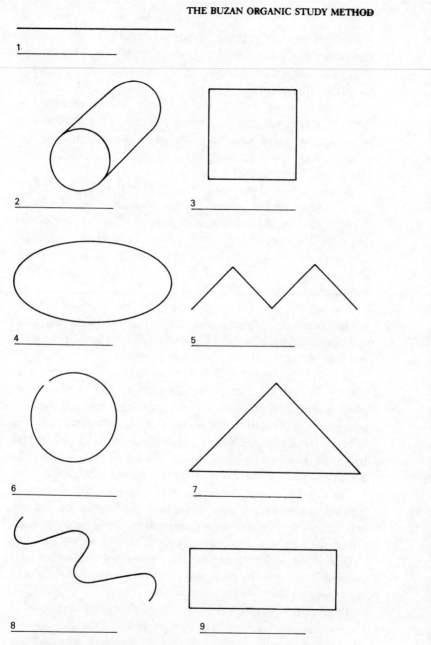

2 _____   3 _____

4 _____   5 _____

6 _____   7 _____

8 _____   9 _____

Fig 46 **Shape recognition.**
Enter the name of the shape of each of the items above next to the
appropriate number. *See text opposite after completion.*

A more abstract example of our general desire to complete things is our universal tendency as children to build up a language that helps us to make sense of, and form completed ideas of, our surroundings.

In study, making a decision about Time and Amount gives us immediate chronological and volume terrain, as well as an end point or goal. This has the added advantage of enabling the proper linkages to be made rather than encouraging a wandering off in more disconnected ways.

An excellent comparison is that of listening to a lecturer. A good lecturer who is attempting to expound a lot of difficult material will usually explain his starting and his ending points and will often indicate the amount of time he intends to spend on each area of his presentation. The audience will automatically find his lecture easier to follow because they have guide-lines within which to work.

It is advisable to define physically the amount to be read by placing reasonably large paper markers at the beginnings and end of the section chosen. This enables the reader to refer back and forward to the information in the amount chosen.

A further advantage of making these decisions at the outset is that the underlying fear of the unknown is avoided. If a large study book is plunged into with no planning, the reader will be continually oppressed by the number of pages he eventually has to complete. Each time he sits down he will be aware that he still has 'a few hundred pages to go' and will be studying with this as a constant and real background threat. If, on the other hand, he has selected a reasonable number of pages for the time he is going to study, he will be reading with the knowledge that the task he has set himself is easy and can certainly be completed. The difference in attitude and performance will be marked.

There are still further reasons for making these time and amount decisions which are concerned with the distribution of the reader's effort as time goes on.

Imagine that you have decided to study for two hours and that the first half-an-hour has been pretty difficult, although you have been making some progress. At this point in time you find that understanding begins to improve and that your progress seems to be getting better and faster.

Would you pat yourself on the back and take a break?

Or would you decide to keep the new and better rhythm going by studying on for a while until you began to lose the new impetus?

Ninety per cent of people asked those questions would carry on. Of those who would take a break, only a few would recommend the same thing to anyone else!

And yet surprisingly the best answer *is* to take a break. The reason for this can be seen by referring back to the discussion in the chapter on Memory and the amount that is recalled from a period of learning. Despite the fact that understanding may be continually high, the recall of that understanding will be getting worse if the mind is not given a break, thus the graph, fig 18, is particularly relevant in the study situation. It is essential that any time period for studying be broken down into 20–40 minute sections with small rests in between. *See fig 19.* The common student practice of swotting five hours at a stretch for examination purposes should become a thing of the past, for understanding is *not* the same as remembering, as all too many failed examination papers give witness.

The breaks themselves are also important for a number of reasons:

1 They give the body a physical rest and a chance to relax. This is always useful in a learning situation, and releases the build-up of tension.

2 They enable recall and understanding to 'work together' to the best advantage.

3 They allow a brief period of time for the just-studied information completely to relate each part of itself to the other part – to intra-integrate. *See fig 21.*

This last point also relates to the Memory chapter and the graph on forgetting as time progresses. During each break the amount of knowledge that can immediately be recalled from the section just studied will increase and will be at a peak as the next section is commenced. This means that not only will more be recalled because the time period itself is best, but also that even more will be recalled because of the rest period.

To assist this even further, do a quick review of what you have read and a preview of what you are about to read at the beginning and end of each study period.

It has taken a number of pages to explain the necessity of deciding on a period of time and on an amount to be covered, but remember that the decisions themselves are extremely brief and will usually become automatic as you near completion of your browse. When these decisions have been made the next step can be taken:

Noting of knowledge on the subject

Having decided on the amounts to be covered, next jot down as much as you know on the subject as fast as you can. No more than two minutes should be devoted to the exercise. Notes should be in key words and in creative pattern form.

The purpose of this exercise is to improve concentration, to eliminate wandering, and to establish a good mental 'set'. This last term refers to getting the conscious mind filled with important rather than unimportant information. If you have spent two minutes searching your memory banks for pertinent information, you will be far more attuned to the text material, and will be far less likely to continue thinking about the strawberries and cream you are going to have after.

From the time limit of five minutes on this exercise it is obvious that a person's entire knowledge is not required on the pattern – the two minute exercise is intended purely to activate the storage system and to set the mind off in the right direction.

One question which will arise is 'what about the difference if I know almost nothing on the subject or if I know an enormous amount?' If knowledge in the area is great, the five minutes should be spent forming a pattern of the major divisions, theories and names etc. connected with the subject. As the mind can flash through information much faster than the hand can write it, all the minor associations will still be mentally 'seen' and the proper mental set and direction will be established.

If the knowledge of the subject is almost nothing, the two minutes should be spent patterning those few items which are known, as well as any other information which seems in any way at all to be connected. This will enable the reader to get as close as he possibly can to the new subject, and will prevent him from feeling totally lost as so many do in this situation.

Apart from being immediately useful in study, a continued practice with patterning information gives a number of more general advantages. First, the individual gains by gathering together his immediate and current state of knowledge on areas of interest. In this way he will be able to keep much more up to date with himself and will actually know what he knows, rather than being in a continually embarrassing position of not knowing what he knows – the 'I've got it on the tip of my tongue', 'if only I could make sense of what I know' syndrome.

In addition this continued practice of recalling and integrating ideas gives enormous advantage in situations where such abilities are essential: examinations, impromptu speeches and answering on the spot questions, to name but a few.

Once the five-minute period is up, the next stage should be moved to immediately.

Asking questions – defining goals

Having established the current state of knowledge on the subject, it is next advisable to decide what you want from the book. This involves defining the questions you want answered during the reading. The questions should be asked in the context of goals aimed for and should, like the noting of knowledge, be done in key word and mind map form. Many prefer to use a different coloured pen for this section, and rather than starting a new map they add their questions to the already existing map on current knowledge.

This exercise, again like that for noting knowledge, is based on the principle of establishing proper mental sets. It should also take not much more than five minutes at the outset, as questions can be redefined and added to as the reading progresses.

A standard experiment to confirm this approach takes two groups of people who are generally equal in terms of age, education, aptitude etc. Each group is given the same study text and is given enough time to complete the whole book.

Group A is told that they are going to be given a completely comprehensive test on everything in the book and that they must study accordingly.

Group B is told that they will be tested on two or three major themes which run through the book, and that they also must study accordingly.

Both groups are in fact tested on the entire text, a situation which one would immediately think unfair to the group that had been told they would be tested only on the main themes.

One might also think that in this situation the second group would do better on questions about the themes they had been given, the first group better on other questions and that both groups might have a similar final score.

To the surprise of many, the second group not only does better on questions about the themes, but they achieve higher total scores which include better marks on all parts of the test.

The reason for this is that the main themes act like great grappling hooks through the information, attaching everything else to them. In other words the main questions and goals acted as associative and linking centres to which all other information became easily attached.

The group instructed to get everything had no centres at all to connect new information to, and because of this were groping with no foundations through the information. It is much like a situation where a person is given so much choice that he ends up making no decision; the paradox where attempting to get everything gains nothing.

Asking questions and establishing goals can be seen, like the section preceding it, to become more and more important as the theory behind becomes better understood. It should be emphasised that the more accurately these questions and goals are established, the more able the reader will be to perform well in the Application section of the Organic Study Method.

Personal Notes

Personal Notes

C: Application

Overview

- Study Overview
- Preview
- Inview
- Review
- Note taking
- Continuing review
- Summary

Study Overview

One of the interesting facts about people using study books is that most, when given a new text, start reading on page one. It is *not* advisable to start reading a new study text on the first page. The following situation is a parallel illustration of this point:

Imagine that you are a fanatic jigsaw-puzzle-doer. A friend arrives on your doorstep with a gigantic box wrapped in paper and tied with string, and tells you that it's a present: 'the most beautiful and complex jigsaw puzzle yet divised by man!'. You thank her, and as you watch her walk away down the front path, you decide that from that moment on you are going to devote yourself *entirely* to the completion of the puzzle.

Before continuing, note in *precise detail* the steps you would take from that point on in order to complete the task.

Now check your own answers with the following list compiled from my students:

1 Go back inside the house.

2 Take off the string.

3 Take off the paper.

4 Dispose of string and paper.

5 Look at the picture.

6 Read the instructions, concentrating on number of pieces and overall dimensions of the puzzle.

7 Estimate and organise amount of time necessary for completion.

8 Plan breaks and meals!

9 Find surface of appropriate dimensions for puzzle.

10 Open box.

11 Empty contents of box onto surface.

12 If pessimistic, check number of pieces.

13 Turn all pieces right side up.

14 Find edge and corner pieces.

15 Sort out colour areas.

16 Fit 'obvious' bits and pieces together.

17 Continue to fill in.

18 Leave 'difficult' pieces to end (for reason that as the overall picture becomes more clear, and the number of pieces used increases, so does the probability increase that the difficult pieces will fit in much more easily when there is greater context into which they *can* fit).

19 Continue process until completion.

20 Celebrate!

This jigsaw analogy can be applied directly to study, in the first instance making it clearer why it is so important not to commence studying on page one, as doing so would be like finding the bottom left-hand corner, and insisting to yourself that the entire picture be built up step by step from that corner only.

What is essential in a reasonable approach to study texts, especially difficult ones, is to get a good idea of what's in them before plodding on into a learning catastrophe. The overview is designed to perform this task, and may be likened to looking at the picture, reading the instructions, and finding the edge and corner pieces of the puzzle. What this means in the study context is that you should scour the book for all material not included in the regular body of the print, using your visual guide as you do so. Areas of the book to be covered in your overview include:

results	tables	subheadings
summaries	table of contents	dates
conclusions	marginal notes	italics
indents	illustrations	graphs
glossaries	capitalised words	footnotes
back cover	photographs	statistics

The function of this is to provide you with a good knowledge of the graphic sections of the book, not skimming the whole thing, but selecting specific areas for relatively comprehensive coverage. *See fig 47.*

It is extremely important to note again that throughout the overview a pen, pencil, or other form of visual guide should always be used.

Fig 47 **Sections of a study text to be covered by overview.** *See text page 139.*

The reason for this can best be explained by reference to a graph. If the eye is unaided, it will simply fixate briefly on general areas of the graph, then move off, leaving only a vague visual memory and an interference to that memory because the eye movement will not have 'registered' the same pattern as the graph.

Fig 48 **Example pattern of graph to be studied.**

If a visual aid is used, the eye will more nearly approximate the flow of the graph and the memory will be strengthened by each of the following inputs:

1 The visual memory itself.

2 The remembered eye movement approximating the graph shape.

Fig 49 **Standard pattern of unguided eye movement on graph causing conflicting memory of shape of graph.**

3 The memory of the movement of the arm or hand in tracing the graph (Kinaesthetic memory).

4 The visual memory of the rhythm and movement of the tracer.

The overall recall resulting from this practice is far superior to that of a person who reads without any visual guide. It is interesting to note that top accountants often use their pens to guide their eyes across and down columns and rows of figures. They do this naturally because any very rigid linear eye movement is difficult to maintain with the unaided eye.

Preview

The second section of study application is the preview – covering all that material not covered in the overview. In other words the paragraphed, language content of the book. This can be likened to organising the colour areas of your puzzle.

During the preview, concentration should be directed to the beginnings and ends of paragraphs, sections, chapters, and even whole texts, because information tends to be concentrated at the beginnings and ends of written material.

If you are studying a short academic paper or a complex study book, the Summary Results and Conclusion sections should always be read first. These sections often include exactly those essences of information that you are searching for, enabling you to grasp that essence without having to wade through a lot of time-wasting material.

Having gained the essence from these sections, simply check that they do indeed summarise the main body of the text.

In the preview, as with the overview, you are not fully reading all the material, but simply concentrating once again on special areas. *See fig 50.*

amount of material to be studied

sections to be covered by preview after overview

Fig 50 **Sections to be covered by preview after overview.** *See text this page.*

The value of this section cannot be overemphasised. A case in point is that of a student taught at Oxford who had spent four months struggling through a 500-page tome on psychology. By the time he had reached page 450 he was beginning to despair because the amount of information he was 'holding on to' as he tried to get to the end was becoming too much – he was literally beginning to drown in the information just before reaching his goal.

It transpired that he had been reading straight through the book, and even though he was nearing the end, did not know what the last chapter was about. It was a complete summary of the book! He read the section and estimated that had he done so at the beginning he would have saved himself approximately 70 hours in reading time, 20 hours in note-taking time and a few hundred hours of worrying.

In both the overview and preview you should very actively select and reject. Many people still feel obliged to read everything in a book even though they know it is not necessarily relevant to them. It is far better to treat a book in the way most people treat lecturers. In other words if the lecturer is boring skip what he says, and if he is giving too many examples, is missing the point or is making errors, select, criticise, correct, and disregard as appropriate.

Inview

After the overview and preview, and providing that still more information is required, inview the material. This involves 'filling in' those areas still left, and can be compared with the filling in process of the jigsaw puzzle, once the boundaries and colour areas have been established. It is *not* necessarily the major reading, as in some cases most of the important material will have been covered in the previous stages.

difficult areas or areas where knowledge not complete

Fig 51 **Sections covered after inview has been completed.** *See text this page.*

It should be noted from fig 50 that there are still certain sections which have been left incomplete even at the inview stage. This is because it is far better to move *over* particularly difficult points than to batter away at them immediately from one side only.

Once again the comparison with the jigsaw puzzle becomes clear: racking your brains to find the pieces that connect to your 'difficult bit' is a tension-producing waste of time, and jamming the piece in, or cutting it with a pair of scissors so that it *does* fit (assuming or pretending you understand in context when *really* you don't) is similarly futile. The difficult sections of a study text are seldom essential to that which follows them, and the advantages of leaving them are manifold:

1 If they are not immediately struggled with, the brain is given that most important brief period in which it can work on them subconsciously. (Most readers will have experienced the examination question which they 'can't possibly answer' only to

find on returning to the question later that the answer pops out and often seems ridiculously simple).

2 If the difficult areas are returned to later, they can be approached from both sides. Apart from its obvious advantages, considering the difficult area in context (as with the difficult bit in the jigsaw) also enables the brain's automatic tendency to fill in gaps to work to greater advantage.

3 Moving on from a difficult area releases the tension and mental floundering that often accompanies the traditional approach.

Fig 52 'Jumping over' a stumbling block usually enables the reader to go back to it later on with more information from 'the other side'. The block itself is seldom essential for the understanding of that which follows it. *See text this page.*

An adjunct to this last point is that it tends to make studying a more creative process.

Looking at the normal historical development of any discipline, it is found that a fairly regular series of small and logically connected steps are interrupted by great leaps forward.

The propounders of these giant new steps have in many cases 'intuited' them (combining left and right brain functions, as outlined in chapter 1), and afterwards been met with scorn. Galileo and Einstein are examples. As they then explained their ideas step by step, others gradually and progressively understood, some early in the explanation, and others as the innovator neared his conclusion.

In the same manner in which the innovator jumps over an enormous number of sequential steps, and in the same manner in which those who first realised his conclusions did so, the studier who leaves out small sections of study will be giving a greater range to his natural creative and understanding abilities. *See fig 53.*

Fig 53 **Historical development of ideas and creative innovations.** *See text page 144.*

Review

Having completed the overview, preview and inview, and if further information is still required, a review stage is necessary.

In this stage simply fill in all those areas as yet incomplete, and reconsider those sections marked as noteworthy. In most cases it will be found that not much more than 70 per cent of that initially considered relevant will finally be used. Then complete your mind map notes.

Noting

Noting while studying takes two main forms:
1 Notes made on the text itself.
2 A growing mind map.

Notes you make in the book itself can include:

1 Underlining.
2 Personal thoughts generated by the text.
3 Critical comments.

straight line mark for important or noteworthy material	curved line mark for difficult or unclear material

Fig 54 **Techniques for marking text**

4 Marginal straight lines for important or note-worthy material.

5 Curved or wavey marginal lines to indicate unclear or difficult material.

6 Question marks for areas that you wish to question or that you find questionable.

7 Exclamation marks for outstanding items.

8 Your own symbol code for items and areas that relate to your own specific and general objectives.

If the book is not valuable, markings can be made in colour codes. If the book is a cherished volume, then markings can be made with a very soft pencil. If the pencil is soft enough, and if a *very* soft eraser is used, the damage to the book will be less than that caused by the finger and thumb as they turn a page.

Mind Mapping structure of the text as you progress through it is very similar to building up the picture of the jigsaw puzzle as you fit in bit by bit. Ideally the bulk of Mind Map noting should take place during the latter stages of study, as in the earlier stages it is very difficult to know that which is *definitely* note-worthy, and subsequently unnecessary noting can be avoided.

It is best to start with a central image that captures the essence of that which you are studying, and from that central image, to branch out with the major sub-subject headings or chapter headings forming the central arms from which the secondary and tertiary levels of your note taking will emanate. *Re-read now 'Noting' section starting on page 71.*

The advantage of building up a Mind Map as you progress through the study text is that you externalise and integrate a lot of information that would otherwise be 'up-in-the-air'. The growing Mind Map also allows you to refer back quickly to areas you have previously covered, rather than having to thumb through pages already read.

It will enable you after a reasonable amount of basic study, to see just where the areas of confusion in your subject are, and to see also where your subject connects with other subjects. As such it will place you in the creative situation of being able to: integrate the known; realise the relevance to other areas; and to make appropriate comment where confusion and debate still exist. The final stage of your study will include the completion and integration of any notes from your text with the Mind Map, which will act as your basis for ongoing study and review.

When you have completed this final stage, you should, as did our imaginery jigsaw puzzle fanatic, celebrate! This may sound humorous, but it is also serious: if you associate the completion of study tasks with personal celebration, the context of your study will become increasingly more pleasant, and thus the probability of your studying far greater.

Once your study programme is well underway, it is advisable to keep enormous 'Central' Mind Maps which summarise and overview the main branches and structures of your subject areas.

Continuing Review

Apart from the immediate review, a continuing review programme is essential, and should be constructed in the light of the knowledge we have concerning memory as discussed in the chapter on Memory.

It was seen that memory did not decline immediately after a learning situation, but actually rose before levelling off and then plummeting.

Fig 55 Graph showing that memory actually rises after learning, before declining sharply. *See text this page.*

This graph can be warped to your advantage by reviewing just at that point where the memory starts to fall. A review here, at the point of highest memory and integration, will keep the high point up for another one or two days and so on as explained on page 58, *see also fig 22.*

Fig 56 **This graph shows how quickly forgetting takes place after something has been learned. It also shows how review can 'warp' this graph to enormous advantage.** *See text this page.*

The Organic Study Method: summary

The entire Organic Study Method must be seen not as a step by step progression, but as a series of inter-related aspects of approaching study material. It is quite possible to switch and change the order from the one given here. The amount to be covered may be decided upon before the period of time; the subject matter may be known before the time and amount are decided upon and consequently the knowledge spray pattern could be completed first; the questions can be asked at the preparation stage or after any one of the latter stages; the overview can be eliminated in books where it is inappropriate, or repeated a number of times if the subjects were mathematics or physics. (One student found that it was easier to read four chapters of post-degree mathematics 25 times per week for four weeks quickly using the survey technique, than to struggle through one formula at a time. He was of course applying to its extreme, but very effectively, the point made about skipping over difficult areas); a preview can be eliminated or broken down into separate sections; and the inview and review can be variously extended or eliminated.

In other words each subject, and each book of each subject, can be confidently approached in the manner best suited to it. To each book you will bring the knowledge that whatever the difficulties, you possess the fundamental understanding to choose the appropriate and necessarily unique approach.

Study is consequently made a personal, interactive, continually changing and stimulating experience, rather than a rigid, impersonal and tiresomely onerous task.

It should also be noted that despite the apparently greater number of 'times the book is being read', this is *not* the case. By using the Organic Study Method you will be on average reading most sections once only and will then be effectively reviewing those sections considered important. A pictorial representation can be seen in fig 57.

Fig 57 'Number of times' book is covered using Organic Study Method. *See text this page.*

By contrast, the 'once through' reader is *not* reading it once through but is reading it an enormous number of times. He thinks he is reading it through once only because he takes in once piece of information after another. He does not realise that his regressions, back-skipping, re-reading of difficult sentences, general disorganisation and forgetting because of inadequate review, result in an actual reading of the book or chapter as many as ten times.

Fig 58 'Number of times' book is covered using traditional 'once through' reading techniques. *See text this page.*

Afterword

As you approach the end of this volume I hope that you will be realising that it is not the end, but the real beginning. With the physical beauty and complexity of your brain, and its enormous intellectual and emotional powers, with your ability to absorb information and to manage the memorisation of that information, and with the new techniques for allowing your brain to express and organise itself in matters which are more comprehensibly attuned to the way you function, reading, studying, learning, and life in general should become what they can be: delightful and flowing processes that bring not pain and frustration, but pleasure and fulfilment.

Personal Notes

Bibliography

Adams, J. A. *Human memory* McGraw-Hill, 1967.

Alexander, F. M. *The Alexander technique: the essential writings of F. Matthias Alexander* ed. E. Maisel. Thames and Hudson, 1974; published originally as *The resurrection of the body* New York: University Books, 1969; Dell Publishing, paperback 1974.

Alexander, F. M. *The use of the self: its conscious direction in relation to diagnosis, functioning and the control of reaction* Methuen, 1931. o.p.

Bergamini, D. *The universe* Time-Life International, 1968.

Bono, E. de *Children solve problems* A. Lane, 1972; Penguin Books, 1972. o.p.; New York: Harper and Row, 1974.

Brown, M. E. *Memory matters* David and Charles, 1977. o.p.; Sphere, 1979; New York: Crane, Russell, 1977.

Buzan, T. *Make the most of your mind* Colt Books, 1977; Pan, 1981.

Buzan, T. *Speed memory* David and Charles, rev. edn. 1977; Sphere, 1974.

Buzan, T. *Speed reading* David and Charles, rev. edn. 1977; Sphere, 1971.

Buzan, T. and Dixon, T. *The evolving brain* David and Charles, 1978; New York: Holt, Rinehart and Winston, 1978.

Cohen, D. H. *The learning child* New York: Pantheon Books, 1972; Wildwood House, paperback 1973. o.p.

D'Arcy, P. *Reading for meaning* Hutchinson for the Schools Council, 2 vols. 1973.

Edwards, B. *Drawing on the right side of the brain.* Boston MA; Houghton Mifflin, St Martin, 1979; Penguin Books, 1981.

Encyclopaedia Britannica 30 volumes E.B., 1974.

Einstein, A. *Relativity* Methuen, 1920. o.p.; rev. edn. paperback 1954; Magnolia, MA: Peter Smith, 1961.

Eyken, W. van der *The pre-school years* Penguin Books, n.e. 1977.

Farb, P. *Ecology* Time-Life International, 1965.

Freire, P. *Pedagogy of the oppressed* New York: Herder, 1970; Sheed and Ward, 1972. o.p.; Penguin Books, 1972.

Gattegno, C. *What we owe children: subordination of teaching to learning* New York: Outerbridge, 1970. o.p.; Routledge, 1971; n.e. paperback 1975.

Hall, J. F. *The psychology of learning* Philadelphia: J. B. Lippincott, 1966. o.p.

Harris, E. E. *Hypothesis and perception* Atlantic Heights, N.J.: Humanities, 1970; Harvester Press, n.e. 1978.

Henry, J. *Essays on education* Penguin Books, 1971. o.p.

Hoggart, R. *The uses of literacy* Chatto and Windus, 1957; Penguin Books 1969.

Holt, J. *How children fail* Pitman, 1970. o.p.; Penguin Books, 1969; New York: Dell Publishing, 1970.

Huxley, A. *The doors of perception* Chatto, 1968; Panther, 1977; New York: Harper and Row, 1970.

Illich, I. D. *Deschooling society* Calder and Boyars, 1971; paperback 1972; Penguin Books, 1971; New York: Harper and Row, 1971.

Illich, I. D. *Celebration of awareness* Calder and Boyars, cased and paperback 1971; Penguin Books, 1976; New York: Doubleday, 1971.

Julesz, B. *Foundations of Cyclopean perception* University of Chicago Press, 1971.

Klee, P. *Notebooks* vol. 1. *The thinking eye* Lund Humphries, 1961; New York: Wittenborn, 1978.

Lapp, R. E. *Matter* Time-Life International, 1965.

Luria, A. R. *The man with a shattered world: the history of a brain wound* New York: Basic, 1972; Cape, 1973; Penguin Books, 1975. o.p.

McCulloch, W. S. *Embodiments of mind* M.I.T. Press, n.e. paperback 1970. o.p.

Maslow, A. H. *Toward a psychology of being* Van Nostrand Reinhold, 2nd edn. paperback 1969.

Maslow, A. H. *Motivation and personality* Harper and Row, 2nd rev. edn. 1970.

Moore, R. *Evolution* Time-Life International, 1969.

Neill, A. S. *Summerhill: a radical approach to education* Gollancz, 1962. o.p.; Penguin Books, 1968.

Neumann, J. von *The computer and the brain* Yale University Press, 1958.

Newson, J. and E. *Patterns of infant care in an urban community* Penguin Books, 1965.

Nourse, A. E. *The body* Time-Life International, 1966.

Pfeiffer, J. E. *The cells* Time-Life International, 1965.

Postman, N. and Weingartner, C. *Teaching as a subversive activity* New York: Delacorte, 1969; Pitman, 1971. o.p.; Penguin Books, 1971.

Razzell, A. G. *Juniors: a postscript to Plowden* Penguin Books, 1968. o.p.

Reimer, E. *School is dead: an essay on alternatives in education* Penguin Books, 1971.

Rudolph, M. *Light and vision* Time-Life International, 1968. o.p.

Saint-Exupery, A. de *The little prince* New York: Harcourt, Brace, 1943; Heinemann, 1945; Piccolo Books, 1974.

Sandström, C. I. *The psychology of childhood and adolescence* Methuen, 1966. o.p.; Penguin Books, 1968.

Sawyer, W. W. *Vision in elementary mathematics* (Introducing mathematics, 1), Penguin Books, 1964. o.p.

Schaff, A. *Introduction to semantics* Pergamon Press, 1962. o.p.

Spencer Brown, G. *Laws of form* Allen and Unwin, 1969; New York: Dutton, 1979.

Starling, E. H. and Evans, Sir Charles *Principles of human physiology* 14th edn. edited by H. Davson and G. Eggleton. Churchill Livingstone, 1968. o.p.

Suzuki, S. *Nurtured by love: a new approach to education* New York: Exposition Press, 1969; Bosworth Press, 1970.

Tanner, J. M. *Growth* Time-Life International, 2nd rev. edn. 1969.

Tolansky, S. *Revolution in optics* Penguin Books, 1968. o.p.

Vaizey, J. *Education for tomorrow* Penguin Books, rev. edn. 1970.

Wilson, J. R. *The mind* Time-Life International, 1966.

Wilson, M. *Energy* Time-Life International, 1965.

Winnicott, D. W. *The child, the family and the outside world* Penguin Books, 1964; Sante Fe, NM: Gannon, 1966.

Yates, F. A. *The art of memory* Routledge 1966: Penguin Books, n.e. 1978; University of Chicago Press, 1966.

Index

Personal Notes

Personal Notes

Personal Notes

Personal Notes

Personal Notes

Personal Notes

Personal Notes

Personal Notes